WINNING AGAIN

A RETENTION GAME PLAN FOR YOUR MOST IMPORTANT CONTRACTS AND CUSTOMERS

Also by Robyn Haydon:

The Shredder Test: A step-by-step guide to writing winning proposals

WINNING AGAIN

A RETENTION GAME PLAN FOR YOUR MOST
IMPORTANT CONTRACTS AND CUSTOMERS

ROBYN HAYDON

Durban Professionals Press

First published 2014
Durban Professionals Press
PO Box 4020
Patterson 3204, Australia

Cover design by RedFred
Book design and typesetting by Sylvie Blair
Author photograph by Stephanie Teh
Book production, copy review and editing by Stephanie Teh
Final editing and proofreading by Kelly Chandler

Trademarks
Ready to Re-compete Program, Contract and Client Leadership Program, Rev Up Your Reporting, Persuasive Tender and Proposal Master Class and Persuasive Speed Writing Program are trademarks of Robyn Haydon. All rights reserved.

All other company, brand and product names are trademarks, registered trademarks or service marks of their respective holders.

Disclaimer
The material in this book is general comment only and neither purports nor intends to be specific advice related to any particular reader. It does not represent professional advice and should not be relied on as the basis for any decision or action on any matter that it covers. To the maximum extent permitted by law, the author and publisher disclaim all responsibility and liability to any person or entity, whether a purchaser or not, in respect to anything and of the consequences of anything done by any such person in reliance, whether in whole or in part, upon the whole or any part of the contents of this publication.

A Cataloguing-in-Publication is available from the National Library of Australia

ISBN: 9780992521622 (paperback)

Acknowledgements

Writing a book is a big project, and I have many people to thank for making it happen.

In particular, I am indebted to the procurement experts and business development leaders who generously let me pick their brains and share some of their insights and stories here. Keep reading to learn more about these clever people.

Thanks also to Paul Hallam and Adam Kurdas of Six Degrees Executive and Richard Hodge of the Brooke Institute for connecting me with some of the fantastic procurement experts I was privileged to talk to.

I am very grateful to the leaders, clients and colleagues who have believed in me, pushed and extended me, and continued to inspire me over the years. Thank you in particular to Glen Makin (who kindly agreed to write the book's Foreword), Andrew Williams, Karen Mahlab, Lisa Fowkes and the late Jason Ashton, and to Christina Guidotti, Matt Church and Peter Cook. In some way, big or small, you have all led — and sometimes dragged — me on the journey to putting this book into the world, and it would not exist without you.

Thanks to Ellinor, Trudi, Molly and the crew at The Decibelles Female Pop Choir for helping me keep some semblance of work/life balance and sense of humour during the months of balancing book writing with a busy consulting practice. You girls rock.

Thanks to Zach, whose already impressive collection of loom bands grew considerably while keeping me company during early morning writing sessions.

And last, but most definitely not least, thank you to Steph, my partner in life and in work, for bringing this project together and for being the best darn illustrator, designer, editor and proof reader ever. And also for keeping me sane, fed and organised, and for putting up with the little bits and pieces of paper all over the place while I talked to my digital recorder incessantly to get everything out of my head. And probably for lots of other things that I don't even notice and have definitely forgotten to mention. You are one in a billion.

Interviews and case studies

The central concepts, methods and models presented in *Winning Again* have been developed in my bid consulting practice. I've spent thousands of hours working as a bid consultant to successful suppliers of complex services, most of whom are competing and re-competing for business that is worth at least $5 million over three years. This work spans hundreds of individual bids and pursuits. To balance these views, I have also sought input and opinions from senior, successful people on both sides of the fence.

The procurement experts I spoke to have worked with some of Australia's largest corporate and government buyers. All have been hugely generous with their time and insights, and were delighted to share what they know to help suppliers to re-compete more successfully.

The procurement experts consulted for *Winning Again* include:

Tehara Wickham, who is Head of Procurement Governance and Engagement at the National Australia Bank – one of Australia's largest buying organisations. Tehara contributed to a major procurement transformation program at NAB three years ago, and now manages a team that oversees the entire procurement and sourcing function at NAB. In this role, she has established governance functions that ensure consistency and has improved the effectiveness of procurement engagement with stakeholders.

Adel Salman, currently Group Procurement Manager for Bega Cheese Ltd, a billion dollar Australian owned and publicly listed dairy company. Adel has held senior procurement roles at Cerebos Ltd, NSW Government, Cadbury Schweppes and GM, and has a proven record of building, managing and inspiring high performance teams in complex organisational and industry contexts.

Neil Hubbard, Procurement Manager at the Metropolitan Fire Brigade (MFB). A Chartered Accountant, Neil held senior procurement roles at Crown Casino for 16 years and also worked as Vendor Manger for Patties Foods.

Craig Amos, Executive General Manager – Commercial at PMP Limited, one of Australia's largest printing and distribution companies. Craig works collaboratively with PMP's suppliers to deliver efficiency gains that help both parties maintain a sustainable business.

Bretton Ackroyd, a partner at the Brooke Institute, a procurement consulting firm working mainly with government entities including the Department of Defence. Bretton's current role involves contract optimisation for complex service delivery contracts, including the use of relational contracting.

Terry Lennard, who is currently working on a Navy ICT procurement program following a military career spanning 43 years of service. Terry has also worked as a senior executive for Western Australia's Department of Health with responsibility for ICT procurement, contracting and support.

On the supplier side, I am very grateful to my clients and other industry leaders, who have allowed me to pepper them with lots of questions and who have generously shared their experiences and wisdom.

Business development success is a competitive and sensitive topic, and one that is challenging for people to talk about publicly. In the face of this, their willingness to share their challenges and successes is an act of true goodwill to others who tread a similar path.

The business development leaders consulted for *Winning Again* include:

Karenza Louis-Smith, CEO of ACSO, a $26 million not-for-profit organisation that is a sector leader in the delivery of forensic community services. Karenza is a hands-on business development leader whose vision for sector transformation in mental health and drug treatment has seen ACSO double its business in the past three years.

Michael Abela, CEO of Skybridge, a $50 million+ privately owned field services company specialising in infrastructure and asset management, installation and maintenance of ICT and solar energy equipment. Skybridge holds contracts with some of Australia's largest private and government buyers, including the National Broadband Network, Optus and the Australian Government. As Managing Director of Gilat Satellite Networks Australia, Michael partnered with Optus to close a multi-hundred million dollar agreement with NBN Co for the First Release Satellite Solution.

Kary Macliver, General Manager Partnerships and Development at Job Futures, a $65 million+ organisation that delivers employment, training and related services. Kary is responsible for driving business growth through new member alliances and tender wins, and at time of writing was leading Job Futures' team in the development and delivery of more than 50 bids for Employment Services (formerly JSA) contracts.

Scott Wright, Manager, Professional Services (Northern Territory) for NEC Australia. Scott is responsible for pursuit management and bid strategy for multiple contracts worth up to $90 million over three years. The Northern Territory is one of NEC's most successful and largest managed services contracts businesses, and the work of the NT team has paved the way for recent wins in similar contracts with government entities in Australia's eastern States.

Brad Richardson, Executive Director of Thinc Group, a management consulting firm specialising in projects. Brad was responsible for building Thinc's national health business and winning significant work on large health infrastructure projects including the $1 billion new Children's Hospital in Perth and the $1 billion Health Infrastructure Program in Canberra.

Catherine Redden and Nik Kilis, Building Sector Commercial Manager and Regional Business Development Manager respectively for global engineering firm Arup in Australasia. Catherine's role oversees project profitability, contractual relationships and operational improvements on existing work. An engineer by profession, Nik loves the challenge of business development and influencing design and is responsible for bringing in $30 million worth of business a year in Victoria alone.

Contents

Contents

Foreword

by Glen Makin

I am delighted to start you off on your journey to Winning Again!

This book offers fresh thinking on an important topic – how to successfully retain business you will have to compete for through enforced, competitive tenders.

As someone who has built – and recently sold – a sizeable business whose revenue depended on winning contracts with corporate and government customers, I've been through my fair share of bids and tenders.

I am an electrician by trade, and first developed a passion for satellite and TV distribution technology while working at Ayers Rock Resort in Central Australia. Moving back to Brisbane, I managed teams of contractors, but in 1999 decided to strike out on my own – just me and my ute, working from the spare bedroom at home. There was a lot of work available for satellite technicians at the time, and even more for good ones. Broadband internet was really starting to get traction in Australia, so I set about educating internet service providers and Telcos about using satellite to deliver their products to regional and remote customers. From this came Skybridge's very first (tiny) delivery contracts.

By 2001, I'd convinced my wife to leave her job, so I really needed to hustle more sales. A company called NewSat was looking for people to install satellite music systems for Woolworths supermarkets around Australia. I gave them a call and two months later, we had a contract worth $800,000. We quickly won another with Satellite Music Australia to roll out a similar system for Coles Supermarkets and Bi-Lo, and Skybridge was on its way.

For the next few years we steadily built our systems and relationships with internet service providers and soon had a sizeable business delivering satellite-based internet to regional and remote areas of Australia. Our first big foray into the procurement world was in 2008, when Skybridge was invited to tender for a commercial contract with Optus. We knew we could do the work, but when the Request for Tender arrived it quickly became apparent that it was going to be a huge task to respond. Luckily, we met Robyn, who had a lot of experience in preparing tender responses of this size. Skybridge won this contract, the first of many we have won while working with Robyn - approximately $100 million worth of business to date (and still counting). By 2009, Skybridge was the ninth fastest growing company in Australia.

Skybridge has always competed against much large organisations, many of them publicly listed, with strong balance sheets and deep pockets. As a smaller player, we've always been the underdog, and the perceived risk of engaging with us has been high. For Skybridge, it was never going to be enough just to meet the basic requirements of the Request for Tender.

Because of this, when selling to procurement, our emphasis has always been on the innovation in what we offer – and particularly how these innovations create value, alleviate risk or save the customer money. As any organisation starts to grow, innovation becomes more difficult. But continuing to innovate in a way that is meaningful to the customer is the only way to keep them – and to convince them that you are still relevant in their world and to their business.

Selling to procurement can be complex and intimidating, and even more so when you already have the business. Many people talk about developing customer 'partnerships', but few are actually achieving this in reality.

Winning Again will show you what it really takes to achieve long term success in these days of compulsory competition, and give you a practical plan to nurture and grow your most important contracts and customers.

GLEN MAKIN
Founder, Skybridge Australia

Introduction

SINCE THE TURN OF the century, business-to-business sales have become heavily procurement driven. So the way we sell has had to adjust.

Most suppliers – even if we don't really like it – have grown accustomed to competing for contracts through formal bids and tenders.

Many have changed the way sales teams are organised and hired extra help to submit proposals.

Through persistence and hard work, you have probably won a number of contracts this way. But you may have also noticed that keeping those contracts is much harder than it used to be.

You might find that customers won't take meetings any more. Everything automatically goes to tender, even the contracts you worked very hard to win. Relationships don't seem quite as important as they once were. Customers are constantly looking around for the next big thing and seem only too happy to move on to get it.

At times, this can feel very disheartening.

But there is a way to keep the customers and contracts that are the most important to you, even though you can't change how you must compete for them.

When business-to-business sales started being dictated to by the procurement process, something interesting started to happen.

Customers now only want to talk to the senior people who sign the contract (the 'revenue owners') or the operations people who deliver the contract. Not the people in between.

This is a high-stakes game and customers want to hear from those who can make decisions and those who know how things run.

Employing salespeople – even senior ones – often doesn't work out, as there is a shrinking role for salespeople to play. Revenue owners have stepped in to take on this role as well as running the business, managing the Board, and dealing with all the other things that being Head of Everything entails.

Welcome to the new world of business-to-business sales, where revenue owners are the primary business developers and contract delivery teams are the primary selling team.

If you're a revenue owner – a senior person who is ultimately responsible for sales – your role has definitely changed. All of a sudden you are Chief Bid Leader and the person responsible for running proposals and pursuits. Sure, you have people to help you, but you're the one in charge.

For many revenue owners, this is a scary and exposed place to be.

Even scarier is that after you bid for and win the contract, all the risk and responsibility moves from you to your delivery team.

During the contract, your delivery team is your primary selling team. For convenience, I'll call this your **contract delivery team**. It might be your bid that got the foot in the door, but your contract delivery team is responsible for keeping the door open.

My first book *The Shredder Test – a step-by-step guide to writing winning proposals* was essentially about how to get your foot in the door without shooting yourself in it.

This book is about what to do when you're inside – how to maintain a long-term place at the table as a preferred supplier.

The good news is that sales is still all about relationships – it's just that the way these relationships are conducted has fundamentally changed.

Your formal bid, proposal, submission or tender response is often the only way to get business these days. Everything you have today will be subjected to regular formal competition – most commonly, every three years.

This means that at the very minimum, you and your contract delivery team need to work hard every day to make sure that you have a story to tell the next time your contract goes out to tender.

So it's time to forget about the 'art of war'. This is a much longer, more detailed and in many ways more transparent game than you may be used to playing.

Business development is not a numbers game when we sell complex services. Instead, it is a game of passion, persistence and insight.

Winning a contract is really just a licence to continually talk to the customer about our new ideas, and the work of retaining an existing customer needs to start well before the Request for Tender.

Something that I've noticed over more than 15 years of working with incumbent suppliers in many different industries is that the most successful ones – the clear winners – share a very clear and focused pattern of behaviour when competing for existing contracts, while others set themselves up to lose.

The difference between the clear winners and those who aren't as successful as they could be is what I call the 'opportunity gap'.

This is the gap between what actually wins business and what we hope will win business. It's the space between the concrete and the conceptual. It's the difference between contract management and contract leadership, between what we're doing now and what we need to do to position ourselves to win again.

A lot of the conversation in business development tends to be about our credentials and how to shape and craft them to suit an opportunity. In fact, actions are more powerful than credentials. Actions show what we are working on next. Credentials only show what we've already done.

Put yourself in the customer's shoes. You're making a buying decision that will affect your organisation's future. Which would you rather hear your current supplier talking about –

what they did during the current contract term, or the great things they will do during the next one?

In this book, you will learn about:

- The opportunity gap: why it exists and how to identify it in yourself, the team or organisation you manage.

- How successful suppliers bridge the opportunity gap to become clear winners, and the four things you must do to position yourself to retain the contracts and customers you can't afford to lose.

- How to lead and manage yourself and your team when you are involved in complex pursuits, bids and proposals, including how to focus your effort where it most matters – on what's going to help you win.

This book is for everyone who does great work and wants to do more. It's about retaining the business you already have through a combination of breakthrough ideas and focused effort.

And here is the good news.

Procurement is not the enemy. In fact, when you already supply complex services to a business or organisation, the customer's procurement team can be a genuine ally in helping you to retain, and even grow, your business.

When it comes to the supply of services, procurement is judged on how well your services help their internal clients to achieve results. When the business loves you, the procurement team will love you. When you help procurement achieve their goals, they will help you achieve yours too. It's a three-way win for everyone.

My hope is that you will find the principles in this book useful as you develop your whole business, not just your most important contracts and customers.

It's good business to be good at what you do. It's good business to strive to be great at it. It's good business to understand what your customers really want, to understand what their business is all about, to know your role in their business, and how you can help them. It's good business to know and implement good practice in your business, including ideas that you come up with yourself and ideas that you've seen others implement. It's good business to try new ideas and to constantly think of new and better ways of doing things.

Some of the ideas you try will be fantastic, win business and hold your market space for many years to come. Others won't be so good. Some of the things you try won't work at all.

But we need to keep moving forward because business never stops and neither do your competitors.

There's no doubt about it, competition can be rough.

No matter how successful you already are, no matter how many great things you've done in the past, there is always tomorrow and the spectre of competition. There is also something very personal about putting new ideas out there for criticism and potential rejection.

A word of encouragement before we start.

I know how intimidating it is to be in a situation where your biggest customer could potentially drop you. I know how angry and defensive people can get while merely considering the possibility.

I'm not out to further complicate a situation that many find complex and intimidating, and then sell you the 'solution'.

Business development should not be complex or intimidating. It should be fun.

It's energising to talk to people whose problems we can solve. It's fun to think of new and better ways of doing things. It is intensely rewarding to deliver something that enriches our lives and our customers' lives.

This book is not designed to scare you, but to empower you.

When everyone in your business is working together, you will win more than your fair share of business in your market and retain your most important contracts and customers. Others have done it and you can too.

Keep these principles at the core of what you do and you'll not only have a business-winning machine, but also you'll have a great business that makes a difference in the world.

And if you're up for that, I'd love to help you to achieve it.

ROBYN HAYDON
www.robynhaydon.com
www.winningwords.com.au

PART 1

The Market

The way sales are transacted in business-to-business markets has fundamentally changed, and business won through formal bids and tenders must be retained the same way. In this section, we explore the evolution of business-to-business sales methods, including competitive tendering, and explain why being the incumbent supplier only gives you an advantage if you choose to use it.

CHAPTER 1

The New World of Business-to-Business Sales

THERE IS NO DOUBT that winning business through a formal bid or tender can be really tough.

First, there's the waiting for the Request for Tender (the briefing document you have to address in your proposal). Then, you have to decipher it and figure out what you need to do to respond. You can't talk to the buyer at this point, because they've gone into probity lockdown. Eventually you submit your proposal. Then there's more waiting until you hear that you've been shortlisted. After that there's a presentation to a bunch of people. One or two may be familiar, friendly faces, but the others you might have never met before and probably will never see again. Then, there's some back and forth negotiation about price and commercial terms and possibly a best and final offer round. And then there's some more waiting.

Finally, you get there. You've won.

And hey, by the way – great job. That certainly wasn't easy.

But there isn't any time to relax and enjoy things. You are straight into delivery, and there is such a lot to do.

At this point, your confidence is at an all-time high. You were the best team for the job. The buyer loved you. Competitors couldn't come close.

And now, you are the incumbent. Nobody can touch you.

Until they can.

When you are the incumbent supplier, the game changes. It's time to level up and face a new sort of competition – with yourself.

When business is won through a competitive procurement process like a formal bid or tender, it must be retained by competing again when the contract term expires.

In this way, being an incumbent supplier is similar to being a politician or other publicly elected official. The difference is that politicians and publicly elected officials go into their jobs with an acute appreciation that they will eventually be up for re-election, and they think constantly about what they need to do to win again.

By contrast, incumbent suppliers tend to see a contract as a gift for life, rather than something that we will eventually have to compete for again.

And it is here that we let ourselves down.

In Australia, voting is compulsory to elect a new federal government. That means every three years, we are treated to an all-out display of politicking designed to win our vote.

It's fascinating to see how politicians behave when they know it's make-or-break time.

Our political representatives absolutely understand that how they are perceived will determine the job they get – if they get one at all – for the next three years or more. Will they be elected? If so, will they be on the winning side or the losing side? How much impact will they really have for their electorate and the causes that they believe in?

During an Australian election, you'll find our politicians frantically tweeting, Facebooking, flying around the country and appearing on any TV program that will have them. Last election, a national TV show ran a hugely popular political interview segment called "I hate you, change my mind". Unbelievably, some of the country's best-known politicians lined up to feature on the show.

Picture the contracts you have coming up for bid soon. You will have four weeks to respond when the Request for Tender comes out.

What are you doing to push your agenda in front of the customer now, before the probity period locks down? What are you doing to boost performance? To innovate? To leverage your advantage as the incumbent and fence off the business from competition?

In most cases, if you're honest, the answer is probably "not as much as we could be doing".

I really wanted to start this book with the section titled Your Message, because having the right message really is the most important contributor to winning again.

Realistically, though, it's impossible to do that effectively without first understanding the environment in which we operate. The procurement model of competition is so ingrained in the way the market works now that any discussion of how and what to sell really needs to start here.

Since 2001, I've run a practice helping companies to compete and re-compete for contracts through formal bids tenders and other written proposals. My background before this is in strategic marketing in business-to-business markets, doing much the same thing. Although I've helped hundreds of clients to find their way through the Request for Tender process, and experienced first-hand the results of procurement processes and decisions, I have always worked on the supply side. So as well as sharing with you what I have learnt over the past two decades about the tendering system, I want you to hear directly from procurement experts who breathe the air on the other side of the fence. You can learn more about these generous people in the Acknowledgements, and you will see their specific comments and insights throughout the book, particularly in the first two sections (The Market and Your Message).

Firstly, some words of comfort. Procurement's processes are designed to be simple for suppliers to follow, otherwise there wouldn't be any competition. This may not mean that you actually find them simple, but they are intended to be as straightforward as possible.

Procurement isn't out to trick suppliers or trip us up. It is their job to engage good suppliers who do great work.

If the voice in your head makes your relationship with procurement sound more complex and adversarial, please try to ignore it. Procurement is not designed to be like that. In fact, the competitive tendering system we have today is designed to remove some of the inequities and inefficiencies of past approaches to business-to-business sales.

Competitive tendering is here to stay. As an incumbent supplier who competes within the system, you need to understand and embrace it to have the best chances of winning again.

Competitive tendering started in the mid-20th century, but really took off in the 1980s when governments in western countries established compulsory competitive tendering for public entities. Governments in the 1980s were swept up in economic rationalism, and concepts like deregulation, privatisation of state-owned industries and a reduction in the welfare state were all popular.

The origins of competitive tendering grew from the idea of 'contracting out' – having private sector contractors carry out work that public sector agencies might otherwise have done internally.

By tendering contracts to specialists, buyers figured it would cost them less and they would be able to take advantage of productivity gains made by suppliers too. On paper, this seemed to make sense.

In Australia, the volume of tenders started off at a fairly modest level in the 1980s, but it doubled in the 1990s as compulsory competitive tendering started to take off. For example, between 1994 and 1999, municipalities in Victoria had to expose first 20 per cent, then 30 per cent and finally half of their annual budgets to tenders.

In around the year 2000, compulsory competitive tendering was replaced by the best value system, which is still in play today. This emphasises the quality and performance of suppliers, not just cost effectiveness, and downplays competition as the prime objective. The number of competitive tenders, however, continued to power on. It had already doubled again in Australia by 2000, and today, the volume of tenders has just exploded as everything from washroom supplies to warships is put out to bid.

So you aren't imagining things if you've noticed this trend in your industry.

We've gone from a time when multimillion dollar contracts were sealed with a handshake, to a time when contracts of much lesser value require much more effort for suppliers to win. For example, at time of writing, the Victorian government required three quotes for any purchase over $25,000 and a formal tender for any purchase over $150,000.

Back when I started in this line of work 20 years ago, tenders weren't the only way that buyers bought things, and the tendering system itself was much simpler.

For starters, there's the workload, which these days can be gruelling to the point of exhaustion.

In 1995, simple quotes were the norm, and Requests for Tender were usually preceded by an Expressions of Interest process, which allowed buyers to scope the market and suppliers to prequalify. These were usually short documents and straightforward for suppliers to complete. Unfortunately, Expressions of Interest seem to be disappearing as fast as the Antarctic ice shelf. Today most contracts go straight to Request for Tender.

Tender documents themselves used to be 80 per cent quantitative: they were mostly about pricing. Now, they are 80 per cent qualitative: there is a huge amount of work to do in answering questions, completing schedules, and presenting information creatively. There once was a time when the submission itself had no limits. Now, there are page limits, word limits, and even character limits as buyers struggle to manage their evaluation workload. Proposals that used to take suppliers maybe a few hours to complete now take days, weeks or months, and often longer.

As a result, many suppliers feel exhausted by the process and now treat proposals as an exercise in paperwork, rather than as an exciting opportunity to win and retain business.

I think this is mostly because it feels like the relationship has been taken out of the equation. But it hasn't.

Despite appearances, business won through competitive tendering is still about relationships – it's just that the way those relationships are conducted has fundamentally changed.

We are moving from an environment where people and personal relationships had a lot of power, to one where ideas and innovation are the primary currency that drives the customer relationship.

To understand how this came about, it's worth reflecting on how business-to-business sales have been carried out in the past, and how they have evolved to where they are today.

When I first started out in sales and marketing, I worked for a business that sold diaries (yes, it was that long ago). This was back in the days of 'relationship selling'.

Our corporate sales manager, let's call her Sharon, was a one-woman charm offensive. The energy and enthusiasm that Sharon had for selling diaries was remarkable. What is most remarkable is that she was able to sustain this energy every single time she made a call – at least five calls a day, five days a week.

Sharon invited me to accompany her on sales calls one day, to see how she did things. As we pulled up in front of each building in her blue Ford Falcon, Sharon would square her shoulders and say, 'Right. We're going to wow them, and we're going to win them". And that's just what she did.

Sharon repeated this cycle, and her mantra, many more times that day and every day that week. Customers loved Sharon, and she made a lot of sales.

As a sales methodology, relationship selling worked brilliantly back in the days when deals – including multimillion-dollar deals – were done on handshake. One of the early advocates of relationship selling, Dale Carnegie, said in his book How to Win Friends and Influence People that:

"The only way on earth to influence others is to talk to them about what they want and show them how to get it."

This is great advice, and still works when we have the opportunity to get in a room with a prospect and sell one-on-one. Unfortunately that happens less often these days.

Relationship selling has always had some limitations, particularly in industries with long sales cycles and many stakeholders. In the 1980s, 'solution selling' started to gain popularity as the go-to methodology for complex sales, particularly in high technology industries. Neil Rackham's iconic sales book *SPIN Selling*, published in 1988, presented a well-research methodology that identified the quality of questions asked by the seller as a huge factor in the buyer's decision to buy. Many thousands of sales people around the world have been trained in the SPIN Selling methodology, and it is still very useful in industries where face-to-face sales remain the norm.

However, face-to-face selling methods are not quite so useful in markets that are heavily procurement driven.

In this new environment, where the relationship between buyers and sellers is conducted at a greater distance than ever before, our approach to business development needs to change.

We are now entering the era of 'innovation selling', where new ideas are what wins business.

In 2011, Matthew Dixon and Brent Adamson set out to discover why some sales reps were still making significant sales throughout the global financial crisis, when so many others were going hungry.

They surveyed thousands of sales representatives across many industries and locations, and their book, *The Challenger Sale*, is the first major evolution of sales theory since SPIN Selling. Here's what they discovered:

> "What sets the best suppliers apart is not the quality of their products, but the value of their insights and new ideas to help customers either make money or save money in ways they didn't even know were possible.
>
> Challenger reps ... teach customers something new and valuable about how to compete in their market. **Our research on customer loyalty ... shows that this is the exact behaviour that wins customers for the long term.**
>
> Challengers are not so much world-class investigators as they are world-class teachers. They win, not by understanding the customer's world as well as the customer does themselves, **but better ... teaching them what they don't know but should.**"

The emphasis is mine, but the inference is clear. Customers value suppliers who come to them continually with new and better ways of doing things.

This is great news for anyone who has to compete for business through formal bids and tenders, particularly when you already have a contract (or contracts) you would like to retain.

As an incumbent supplier you have three starting advantages that you can exploit.

1. You have knowledge of how the customer does business. You **know more** than anybody else about how they operate, at least the part of their operation that involves your area of experience and expertise.

2. You have access. You can get deeper inside the organisation, in a way that competitors who are not working with the customer would find very difficult to replicate. This means you have the ability to **learn more** about their issues, and how you can help.

3. You have an audience. You have a customer who is already paying you money to do things, who you can **influence more** about how those things can be done better. By applying your expert lens to their problems and by finding opportunities, including those they are as yet unaware of, you can also help them to see how they can run their business more efficiently and compete more effectively.

Unfortunately, most incumbent suppliers don't leverage these advantages nearly as well as they could, and many don't start actively planning how to retain a particular contract or customer until the Request for Tender has already landed.

As a result, I have been invited to run bid strategy sessions with boardrooms full of anxious people who are acutely aware that they now only have only have four weeks to get their act together. I can see exactly what parts of their story are missing after spending a day trying to plan a winning response with these teams, based on what I know from working with successful teams about what clients are looking for from incumbent suppliers, and what will actually win the business. It's frustrating for them, and for me, that there's so much more that could have been done, if only we had started early enough.

Essentially, this book – and the work that I do now getting organisations ready to re-compete for business – was born out of that frustration, and the desire to help more suppliers create a sustainable competitive advantage that safeguards their most important contracts and customers.

Every contract changes hands at some point. Whether that's into your new and improved hands, or someone else's hands, is really up to you.

Procurement has an obligation to go to market; not necessarily every time a contract expires, but regularly enough that they understand what the market is able to offer. Things change rapidly, and buyers are responsible for getting the best deal and the best result for their organisation.

Because of this, bids and tenders are here to stay. They may look like paperwork, but they certainly don't behave that way. Tender documents, like Requests for Tender, are simply a convenient way to collect comparable responses from different suppliers. And customers expect much more than a tick-the-box response, particularly from their incumbent suppliers.

Possibly the most common complaint I heard from the procurement experts I interviewed from this book – all of whom were generous with their time and insights, because they really do want to help you to win again – is that incumbent suppliers don't bring enough sustained effort, energy and insight to the engagement.

Procurement expert Bretton Ackroyd recalls a time when he worked on a complex Australian Navy IT procurement, where the Navy appointed an IT supplier to help define its requirement, provide project management and deliver an IT infrastructure program.

Halfway through the acquisition contract, the Navy went back to market because the preferred IT supplier wasn't delivering the promised expertise. "They pitched their A-team upfront, but gave us the B-team instead," says Ackroyd.

Tehara Wickham, head of Procurement Governance and Engagement at National Australia Bank, agrees that it's common to see junior people from the supplier organisation throughout the course of the contract and then be inundated with requests for meetings from "every man and woman from the CEO onwards" at the end of the contract, during renewal or at tender time. By then, she says, it's too late.

Suppliers need to have been building those relationships and strengthening multiple levels of engagement throughout the contract, not just bringing in the big guns at the end in an effort to impress the buyer.

Likewise, procurement expert Neil Hubbard says that most suppliers will only give procurement what they say they want. Because he expects more than this, a major part of his team's day-to-day work involves working closely with suppliers and encouraging them to be more proactive.

"The shift has moved away from finding a supplier that can do a job for a price to finding a supplier that can do the job that we don't know we want. We only know what we know. We don't know what we don't know," Hubbard explains. Imagine the efficiencies that could be gained for Hubbard if his suppliers already came to the table with a 'challenger' mindset.

If you have a contract that you've held for a while and it comes up for bid again, other people are going to want it. There might be three competitors, six, 12, 24, or even more. It can feel intimidating as the numbers grow.

While we are busy delivering, competitors are upping their game and figuring out ways to take us out.

Competitors are hungry, and we need to stay hungry too.

I meet many suppliers who work very hard, but don't realise that they are only really delivering on the customer's basic expectations. Essentially, they are just doing what they are being paid for, and even if they are doing this exceptionally well, it isn't enough to win again.

I live in Melbourne, and recently needed to stay in Sydney on business for a few days. It was Mardi Gras time and accommodation was in short supply, so I was only able to get the hotel I wanted for two nights before I had to move on.

The second place wasn't exactly five-star, and when I got into the shower in the morning I had company – there was a tiny cockroach sharing the stall with me. I'm not a huge fan of bugs, but hate the thought of getting rid of them even more. So I turned on the shower, tried not to freak out and kept one eye on what he was up to.

The poor little guy was really struggling. He was going up and down the wall, trying to get away from the water spray and fell a couple of times, but managed to get back up again. And although I wasn't that thrilled to see him there, by the end of the five minutes I was pretty impressed by how damn hard he was working. In the end, my shower companion was trapped up the top and it was obvious that he wasn't going to be able to get to a nice dry space. Just as I was about to switch the shower off, he fell and went down the plughole.

Before he had the misfortune to run into me, that little bug probably thought "Hey, I've got the place to myself. I can hang out here for a while. It's pretty nice in here." And then all of a sudden he found himself in the equivalent of a monsoon.

I don't want to see that happen to you.

Failure is not an option, but it is a reality.

This is a truth rarely acknowledged or talked about in the world of sales and business development, where the only conversation you will ever hear is the one about winning and success.

Yet the prospect of loss is the ugly spectre that hangs over everything we do, and past losses we haven't grieved for and learned from can actually prevent us from doing our best work with the customers we have today.

I am neither trained nor qualified in psychology but have always been fascinated by how people behave when they are under stress. In my line of work I have spent years up close and personal with people while they grapple with the hugely difficult task of bidding for business that means their job, their team's jobs, or even the future of their company.

What I have noticed is that the fear of loss is paralysing for some of these people, while it is the energy and enthusiasm created by the thought of winning –and beyond this, the idea of doing great work that makes a difference on the world – that empowers others to succeed.

Anxiety is a gnawing feeling of worry, nervousness, or unease about something with an uncertain outcome. Knowing that an important contract or customer might go elsewhere can put us in a state of anxiety for a long period of time.

Sustained anxiety causes a range of unwelcome effects – from heart disease to depression – by keeping us in a state of permanent 'fight or flight'.

In the workplace, anxiety presents in many ways that mask what it really is: fear that derives from a sense of powerlessness and the spectre of impending loss. In boardrooms and in bid team 'war rooms', I've seen anxiety show up as arrogance, bullying, lying, dissembling, blind faith, or bluster. Other times anxiety will be cloaked in busy-ness or other forms of reality avoidance.

There is no doubt about it – losses hurt, and when you've always been on top, the only way to go is down.

My son, who is in primary school, loves maths (go figure). Like a lot of kids where we live, he is part of the Mathletics competition at school, which encourages kids to practice their maths online.

Maths is something that comes easily to him and that he is pretty good at it. Since he started Mathletics, he had always been pretty much top of the ladder. One day, he came home from school looking very sad. When I asked him what was wrong, he said, "I was number one on the Mathletics ladder, and now I'm number four." It hadn't even occurred to him that this could happen. He had no frame of reference for the concept that he might not always be on top.

If you have ever lost an important contract or customer, I really feel for you.

I have worked in this game a long time and see many people struggling with unacknowledged grief for past business losses. Sometimes the wounds are fresh and raw. Other times, scar tissue has built up to cover the wound, but it is clear that the loss still affects them.

None of us are robots. We are people with feelings. Losing a customer or contract creates hurt and fear, both of which are huge drags on our creativity, energy and enthusiasm — the very things that we need the most when we need to compete again. Unacknowledged grief is a bomb waiting to go off – somewhere, sometime when you least need and expect it.

Before you delve too far into this book, consider whether the prospect of loss, or your experiences of loss, might affect your ability to move forward today. If you've ever lost a piece of business that was important to you, please give yourself the opportunity to grieve for it. Really feel what happened and then let it go with gratitude.

There are lessons in loss, and one of the most important is to be thankful for and work hard to retain the business that we have today. Being aware that loss is a possibility – and without being scared of it —will drive you to think more broadly and bring new ideas to fruition.

This book sets out the program that will help you to get ready to re-compete for your most important contracts and customers.

At the very least, your Ready-to-Re-compete Program will act as a life raft to get you through the choppy waters of enforced competition. At its very best, this program could be the game-changer that dramatically boosts the value of what you deliver to all your customers.

And the very act of developing and delivering this program will help you to take your power back.

Picture your most important contract or customer – the one you absolutely can't afford to lose. Calculate how much time you have left before the Request for Tender hits.

And let's get you ready to re-compete.

Chapter summary – The New World of Business-to-Business Sales

☑ **Competitive tendering is here to stay.** When business is won through formal bids and tenders, it must be retained the same way.

☑ **Contracts need to be led, not just managed.** Customers expect much more than just baseline delivery of the contract from their incumbent suppliers.

☑ **Ideas and innovation are the primary currency of contemporary customer relationships:** personal relationships are far less important than they used to be.

☑ **As the incumbent supplier you have three starting advantages:** you know more about the customer, have access to learn more and can influence more than competitors can.

☑ **Unacknowledged grief from past losses creates fear that holds us back from fulfilling our potential,** and depletes the creativity, energy and enthusiasm you need to compete and win again.

CHAPTER 2

Getting Ready to Re-compete

WHEN YOU DO GOOD work and want to do more of it, it's a great achievement to win a contract that allows you to use your expertise in the service of others.

Often, too, there is a huge sense of relief that the selling process is over.

In fact, it is never truly over. In many ways, your hard work is just beginning.

Re-competing successfully when you already have the business means working on projects that will create customer value, and this work needs to start well before the contract's use-by date.

The procurement experts I spoke to for *Winning Again* consistently told me that when it comes time to re-compete, only about half of their incumbent contract holders will actually retain the contracts they worked hard to win.

And the reason might surprise you.

It's not always because the incumbent is doing a poor job with the contract. In fact, they're often doing quite a good job. The reason is that they're still doing the **same** job.

And this just doesn't meet a buyer's expectations any more.

A contract isn't a gift for life, but an invitation to keep on evolving and doing things better

Even when there is an option for the buyer to renew the contract, it's dangerous to assume that the renewal will happen automatically. Think of your contract end date as more of a use-by date – a hard deadline by which you need to have a compelling strategy to win the customer all over again.

In our personal lives, most of us have contracts that we would rather not put too much effort into. These often roll over automatically, or are renewed with very little effort on our part.

I once went three months before I realised that my phone was out of plan and was therefore still paying for a handset that was fully paid for. I had to call my provider to get my rate reduced and my money back. Likewise, when insurance is up for renewal, we are often happy enough just to pay the invoice, rather than researching other options.

The consumer businesses we buy from understand this and set things up that way. Good for them – they are the ones in charge.

But when **you** are the supplier and selling to procurement, the situation is very different. The buyer sets the contract and the terms. Even when there is an option to renew, it's their option – not yours.

Because of the way we see contracts operating in our personal lives, we sometimes tend to assume that 'renewal' means 'rollover', but this is a mistake.

Rather than a rollover, a more useful way of thinking about your contract end date is that it's an opportunity for renovation, redevelopment and reinvigoration.

Scott Wright is responsible for pursuit management and bid strategy for NEC's $90 million managed services contracts business in the Northern Territory. In Scott's experience, winning again is a direct result of active contract leadership from day one, constantly finding ways to add value over the term with the impending competitive tender in mind.

NEC is the market leader in the managed services sector and Scott has seen first-hand that customers can become complacent even with a supplier which provides a high quality service. He explains:

> "The risk is that because you have delivered what they want, they believe any company will do the same. So meeting the contract obligations is only the start, and our whole organisation must be committed to exceeding the customer's expectations through the lifecycle of the contract."

Scott's most successful contract retention strategies have been to periodically realign NEC's delivery teams to address changes in the client's organisational structure, and to pursue contract variations that benefit the client by keeping the service relevant to their changing requirements. In one case, Scott and his team put forward a proposal which offered the client – a government department – better value for money, while also delivering operational savings for NEC by transferring work from Melbourne to a Darwin subcontractor. Reputation is always an issue for government and this idea was particularly appealing because it delivered work to local Darwin people. As a result, NEC's contract was extended by a further 18 months. In another case, Scott and his team achieved a 12-month contract extension by undertaking an extra project to migrate a customer's mail platform without increasing their costs.

Why it's good to get comfortable with being uncomfortable

Most successful suppliers tend to trade off their experience and past achievements. Achievements are great, but like trophies in a trophy cabinet, they eventually start to gather dust and cobwebs.

Being 'number one' is a dangerous position to occupy. When you're number one the market won't give you something to aim for — you need to keep creating this yourself.

Bill Gates once said: "Success is a lousy teacher. It seduces smart people into thinking they can't lose."

In my local area, there's a restaurant with a sign proudly proclaiming 'Food Shop Hygiene Shop of the Year'. In huge letters underneath it also says '2000'. The award was a great achievement at the turn of the century, but for customers who might consider eating there today it would be better to see no award at all than to see this very outdated claim.

Every time I read a proposal or tender response that mentions the supplier's 300 years of experience, but doesn't elaborate on how the customer will benefit from this experience (and this happens quite often) it makes me shed tears of frustration.

If you have 300 years of combined experience, that's a heck of a lot of knowledge sitting in your organisation that the customer would love to take advantage of. The problem is, you need to tell them exactly how.

Figuring out how to explain the value of what they do to customers is a problem that regularly occupies the minds of successful business development leaders, such as those I interviewed for this book.

Successful business development leaders know that there is a delicate balance between past achievements and experience, and presenting something that's new, fresh and exciting for a customer.

They get that customers are only really interested in their team's 300 combined years of experience if it means that they are using this experience to do something interesting and valuable right now: turning their knowledge into future results.

Becoming a long-term supplier of choice

It's no longer enough just to be a good supplier. We need to strive to become great suppliers, and this doesn't just mean being great at what we already do for our customers.

Something that I've noticed over many years of working with incumbent suppliers in many different industries is that the most successful ones share a very clear and focused pattern of behaviour when re-competing for existing contracts, while others set themselves up to lose.

The most successful suppliers are those that I call the 'clear winners'.

For me, the term clear winner describes the mindset of the individual business development leader – who will eventually be the bid leader – as well as the course of action that the organisation follows to win and retain business.

Here's how business development leaders demonstrate the mindset of a clear winner.

- Clear winners love what they do and speak eloquently about their business and its opportunities.

- Clear winners can see the big picture and have great ideas with the potential to deliver genuine value for their customers. They focus on serving their customers first and themselves second.

- Clear winners are already successful, and because they have already experienced the benefits of success, they are keen to experience more.

- Clear winners are truly excited about the opportunity to serve customers. They see this as a privilege and not just a 'numbers game'.

- Clear winners believe that there is always a better way of doing things, even when there are already great at what they do.

- Clear winners have a lot on (like everyone else) but always seem to manage to focus on just the right thing. You'll never hear them complain about being 'busy' – instead, they are energised by the work they're doing.

- Clear winners take responsibility for their ideas, for the work we do together, for their actions and the outcomes. They do what's necessary and don't make excuses.

- Clear winners want to do good in the world. Whether they're in business for profit or not-for-profit, they want to leave their part of the world better off than when they started.

- Clear winners seem lucky – others might say that they are 'on a roll' – but that's because they are doing what they love to do, and winning business they deserve to win.

If this sounds like you, that's fantastic. You already have the attitude it takes to be a clear winner. This book will help you with everything else.

The methodology I'm about to walk you through describes the specific course of action you can take as an incumbent supplier to emerge as the clear winner when you need to win again.

These principles apply to winning a contract for the first time too, but become even more important when you are looking to stamp your authority on a contract you already have, and help the customer understand why they should stick with you for the long term.

Your energy, enthusiasm and effort are the things you have most control over in this equation.

The opportunity gap exists between 'focus day-to-day' and 'improve day-to-day'. Most incumbent suppliers tend to concentrate their effort on management tasks during the contract, while clear winners largely invest in leadership and development work.

So it's useful to think of this as an effort scale – where you've achieved 100 per cent effort at the top (when you get to "build their future)" but only about 60 per cent effort below the opportunity gap (if you stick to "focusing day-to-day").

Figure 1: Clear winners prioritise leadership tasks that build the customer's future and their world, and improve day-to-day delivery.

The opportunity gap – from customer and contract management to customer and contract leadership

Let's look at the issue of management first.

Ignore

For some suppliers, the excitement of winning the contract soon wears off. They get distracted by shinier opportunities and as a result they basically **ignore** the contract.

If you've won a contract, but then spend all your time chasing other business, your chances of retaining that contract are only 100 to 1.

You cannot expect any advantage from being the incumbent supplier. You are simply the same as anybody else (or maybe a little worse off).

Assume

This type of supplier puts in slightly more effort. Let's say you've won the contract and embedded it into your business and operations, and it seems to be ticking over ok.

Basically, though, if you're honest, it's not getting very much attention. You just **assume** you will retain it. While your energy isn't distracted, like the first supplier, it's not completely on the job either.

For a reasonably smooth-running contract – one that you're not putting a lot of time and effort into – your chances of retaining it are only about 50 to 1.

These are pretty uncomfortable odds, and hopefully you feel that they don't apply to you. So let's move to a scenario that may sound a little more familiar.

Focus day-to-day

You've just won a new contract. It's important to you. You're not looking elsewhere and you don't ignore it. You **focus on day-to-day delivery.**

You and your team work hard and do a good job. You might expect that this is all you need to do to retain the contract. Unfortunately, that's not quite true either.

This is what you are paid to do. You are paid to deliver on the contract. You are paid to focus on day-to-day delivery.

If this is all you are doing, your chances of retaining that contract are about 25 to 1.

This is because management tasks that focus on day-to-day delivery, even at a high standard, are just a baseline expectation when it comes time to compete again.

Good performance does give you some advantage as the incumbent supplier, but you haven't yet positioned yourself yet as the clear winner.

As Figure 1 shows, the opportunity gap exists between 'focus day to day' and 'improve day to day'.

When we start to look at everything that sits above the opportunity gap, things start to get a lot more interesting. It's here that we start to actively lead the contract, rather than just manage it.

Improve day-to-day

One obvious thing to do, instead of just focusing on day-to-day delivery, is to **improve day-to-day delivery**: to do more than the customer expects you to do.

When you're not just delivering the baseline expectation but improving on it, you increase your odds of winning. There are two ways to do this: through continual improvement and by embedding best practices from the wider market.

Do this well, and in a competitive field of 100 your odds have improved to about 10 to 1.

When I share these odds with people, they often find them quite confronting. Typically, they will wonder: "Why aren't my odds better than 10 to 1? I'm the incumbent. I'm doing a good job. I'm continually improving."

You might guess what the answer to this will be.

Unfortunately, continual improvement, while important, is also a baseline expectation these days. If you deliver a large contract, you are almost certain to be quality accredited, or have a quality program that contains a continual improvement cycle. So continual improvement is something that customers also expect from their suppliers.

Some improvement is definitely better than just meeting the baseline, even if you are doing this well. However, it is never going to be enough when challengers who have nothing to lose can charge in brandishing a shiny picture of what the customer's rosy future would look like working with them instead. You still need to do better.

When a customer buys from a supplier, they expect that they are getting the best solution in the market. They are also sacrificing other options.

It's a big ask for anyone to do this over a sustained period, simply based on faith and good relationships. That's one reason why buyers regularly check the market.

Embedding industry best practice into your service delivery model is a form of reassurance that what you're delivering remains contemporary and relevant. This means looking further afield to identify what others are doing, and figuring out how you can introduce this to your contract or customer.

Improve their domain

Something that far fewer suppliers think about is not just how to improve what we ourselves deliver, but also how to **improve the customer's domain** – to get results that serve the customer's agenda and resonate with their larger business goals.

Often, when we deliver a pitch or tender response, we simply advance our own agenda. We expect to get praise for things we do basically for ourselves.

In long-term sales, we really need to understand where we fit into the customer's world, to reframe our achievements in a way that resonates with the customer and to arm our customer advocates with a story that they can sell for us in their own organisation well before any tender documents are released.

If we do that successfully, our chances of retaining the contract are closer to 5 to 1. These are much better odds, but there is still one more thing that very few suppliers do successfully: something that can really leverage our chances of success in this game.

Build a better future

If you can show the customer how you will create a sustainable future – one that solves their problems, achieves their goals, helps their customers and makes the world a better place – then your odds of winning that contract improve dramatically, and have now gone up to 2 to 1.

There may still be a challenger out there who can put up a decent fight, but you will have done everything you can to safeguard that business from competition.

So here are the top four things that will help you and your team to get serious about retaining and growing your most important contracts and customers.

1. **Innovation:** You're the expert, and the customer expects you to build a picture of how their future might look like if they continue to work with you. This is strategic work that involves building new things: fascinating and inspiring stuff, but also time consuming and difficult. If you don't start thinking about innovation early enough, it doesn't get done at all.

2. **Continual improvement** and **best practice:** You are expected to work on day-to-day improvements that make the most of the money the customer is are paying you today. This means delivering continual improvement in contract

and service delivery. It also means looking further afield to identify best practices and incorporate them into your work with the customer.

3. **Customer advocacy:** The customer expects to see immediate results that make a difference in their world. This means understanding their objectives, and how your work fits with their objectives. It also means being able to frame your ideas and achievements in customer terms – the work of customer advocacy.

4. **Operational excellence:** Of course, you must achieve the results you are being paid for, and meet service level agreements, key performance indicators and targets with a minimal amount of aggravation and noise.

When you do all these things, and reach the top of the effort scale, you are truly leading, not just managing the customer relationship. While a competitor could still come in and trump your offer, it is far less likely, and you will know that you've done everything in your power to win again.

Developing a custodian mindset

When you have an important contract or customer and you plan to work with them for a long time, something else that helps to get your head in the right space is to think of yourself as the custodian of that piece of business.

In practical terms, this means establishing sustained and effective engagement over the course of the contract, not lumpy and ineffective engagement that is artificially tied to the procurement cycle.

The way we engage with the customer is often haphazard. There's the initial fever-pitch nervous energy when submitting the Request for Tender, a flurry of work when getting the contract set up, and then a flat line of delivery over the course of the contract until the fever of the Request for Tender hits again.

Of course, some people will argue that the procurement environment sets things up that way. Bid, deliver and bid again. That might be what the cycle looks like, but it doesn't mean you have to buy into it. In fact, if you want to retain the work, it is essential that you don't.

So, you have temporary ownership of a customer or contract. Do you and your team think more like tenants or custodians of the business?

If you've ever rented a property, then you've been a **tenant** – signed a contract and exchanged some cash for a place to live or work.

I've rented properties and been a landlord myself. One tenant was constantly delinquent on his rent, to the point that our agent had to send him a legal letter every month. The tenant always paid the day before it went to court, causing everybody unnecessary stress. When we finally issued a notice to vacate, we received a letter from him saying how much he loved the property and felt like it was his home, and please could he be allowed to stay!

There are direct parallels between the way bad tenants like this one behave, and the way bad suppliers behave when they get to the end of the contract and are threatened with losing it.

Damage control is only a last resort, and you don't want to get to this point when you have an important contract or customer in your care.

In contrast to tenants paying for temporary use of a property, owners of properties often see themselves as **custodians**.

If you've ever watched renovation shows on TV – particularly the ones where someone falls in love with an old manor house and spends an extortionate amount of money conserving it – you've seen the custodianship mindset in action.

To me, some of these places look like they could do with a bulldozer. But to their owners, renovating the property in the most historically accurate way possible is an important investment. They recognise that many people have lived there before them, and that many others will live there afterwards. They see their custodianship as part of a continuum.

On one TV program, a couple discovered that the 'barn' attached to their Georgian manor was actually an early 15th century dwelling with national significance. Had it not been dated by an expert, this humble building probably would have been demolished because it only had a couple of years left before it fell down on its own. Instead of being exasperated by the cost of the work, which, let's face it, was significant, the owners were proud to have the opportunity to conserve the building for future generations.

Brad Richardson of Thinc Projects believes that custodianship of a project is a key competitive advantage for his business. In a buoyant labour market, the client often loses its development manager or internal lead to other roles, and Brad and his team will be the only consistent thread on the project from start to finish. Thinc Projects worked on the Darwin Waterfront for six years, during which time the client representative changed many times.

"By the end of that job we were the only ones [who] actually knew what happened right back at the start," Brad says. Long after he had moved on to other work, Brad was still fielding calls to locate emails and correspondence that explained particular decisions. Fortunately, Thinc's quality assurance program prioritises filing of documents and records, and this, combined with Brad's own project memory, meant he was always able to help.

The custodian mindset in action

Every piece of business changes hands at some point. Whether into your new and improved hands, or someone else's, is really up to you.

As the incumbent supplier, you are either building something or doing something for the customer. Most likely, this is just one of many things they do in their business. Your job is to add to their business and improve it in some way.

When we treat the relationship like a tenancy – when we do the minimum required of us –we're no better than any other supplier, and it's unlikely that we will get the opportunity to continue. Our relationship is simply transactional.

When we act like custodians though, it's easy for the customer to see our investment of time, energy and enthusiasm as a true strategic partnership in their business.

Incumbent suppliers who act like tenants	Incumbent suppliers who act like custodians
Have a transactional 'management' focus	Have a strategic partnership and 'leadership' focus
Obsess about the work	Obsess about the customer's business
Do good work every day	Do good work today, and better work tomorrow
Are reliable and predictable	Are invaluable and innovative
Trade off their track record	Trade off what they are building
Are better than competitors	Have no direct competitors
Make their contract operate better	Help the customer's business operate better
Deliver what the customer wants and expects	Deliver what the customer doesn't yet know they need
Are only comfortable working with what's concrete and absolute	Are comfortable working with the conceptual and abstract

The good news is that customers often have a vested interest in keeping their existing suppliers, although they do need good reasons to justify why you should stay.

All the procurement experts I spoke to said that in general their preference would be to retain an existing supplier, because of the costs of change.

Adel Salman says that the best way to retain business is to be a great supplier, but is quick to add that being a great supplier doesn't just mean offering to do more of what you are doing today.

While an incumbent's proposal should recognise the history of the relationship, it also needs to explain what you have discovered throughout that relationship, and what yet to come. Because of this, an incumbent's proposal should look quite different to someone who is new to the business. "If it doesn't," says Salman, "then you haven't done your job."

When the customer goes out to market they are actively evaluating other options, so it's important to make sure your proposal focuses on the future.

For example, Richard is a partner in a professional services firm that operates in a very specialised market. Richard and I met socially, and when he heard about the work I do, he shared a wonderful success story. It turned out that just recently, one of the largest customers in Richard's market (for whom his firm was one small supplier among many) had put its work out to tender. The customer wanted a single firm to manage all its work, including all its existing and new business.

This was a once in a lifetime opportunity, and Richard and his firm badly wanted to win. They devoted a team of eight senior people, including partners, to the bid for six weeks – the first time they had ever fielded such a large bid team. Richard and his team did not take the customer for granted. They thought hard about what they could offer and devised an innovative way to structure their service delivery model and their fees to offer value for money. Their bid was successful and they won all the business.

One of the interesting things Richard learned in the tender debrief is that the buyer had made a very deliberate decision to not consider previous relationships and to award the work based solely on what was presented in the tender submission.

In a tender evaluation, a number of people will sit on the evaluation panel. Some may know and care about you, but the majority probably won't.

Even when you have done great work all along, it is dangerous to assume that the evaluators know who you are, or that they will advocate for you if you gloss over information or are sloppy in what you choose to tell them.

Procurement expert Tehara Wickham understands that the procurement process is difficult for incumbent suppliers to go through. She finds that many incumbents assume that the customer knows them, and as a result don't go into enough detail about what they do.

"Time and time again we have to go back to those suppliers and explain that we're facilitating this as an independent process," she says. "You've got to assume that we know nothing, and tell us everything that you want us to know."

Wickham and her team have had to have some very direct conversations with incumbent suppliers whose bids don't measure up and who, as a result, are about to be removed from the short list. Despite the inevitable damage control and rescue effort that follows, the initial impression that this creates is distinctly unfavourable.

As a business development leader, Michael Abela of Skybridge has sat on the other side of this table.

"Re-tendering is the hardest sales process of all," Abela says. "It's a little bit like going for a job you already have, with a boss who is asking you to tell him what you're good at."

Skybridge once lost a tender with a longstanding customer after delivering a significant portion of a national program to install television set-top boxes in pensioners' homes during the switchover to digital television. Each parcel of work was tendered on a region-by-region basis, with the biggest regions last.

In the lead up to one of the largest tenders, the customer publicly acknowledged Skybridge as its most successful contractor. Then Skybridge lost the tender, receiving feedback that there was a lack of confidence in its ability to deliver.

It's an understatement to say that Abela and his team were astounded by this outcome.

"There [was] an absolute incongruence in how they would come to that conclusion based on how strong our past delivery had been," Abela says.

What happened? Well, it was a large and important tranche of work. The winning supplier's tender went into detail about how the work would be delivered, while Skybridge did not. In the two years preceding the tender, Skybridge had completed about 300,000 installations, but the customer evaluated only the tender response. As a result, it appeared that the competitor had a better appreciation of how to deliver the work – despite the fact that they had much less experience.

This decision really hurt Abela, but it permanently changed the way he and his team approached bidding for business. They are now aware of the need to tell the whole story, including all the detail of how they will deliver; not to rely on past successes; and to temper confidence with a strong dose of gratitude and humility.

When the next tranche of digital switchover work was put to tender, Skybridge won. "The customer said they had never seen a better presented tender, and we were so clearly the choice that it was a pleasure for them to give it to us," Abela says.

Planning and projects help you to build positioning

In my experience, winners do not emerge in the time it takes to respond to a Request for Tender. Selling to procurement might look like it's all about paperwork, but actually it's all about positioning.

While writing this book two of my clients were announced as big winners in the Department of Health's sector reforms of mental health and alcohol and drug treatment in Victoria. Both had existing business in this market, and a lot to lose.

The first, a consortium of two longstanding and well-respected treatment providers, grew its business in all the metropolitan Melbourne regions that it pitched for. The second was ACSO, whose CEO Karenza Louis-Smith is quoted throughout this book. ACSO won intake and assessment services across both drug treatment and mental health services in regional areas of Victoria, a significant chunk of new business that added 30 per cent to its annual operating budget and means it was able to employ more than 50 extra staff.

Both organisations had worked for a long time on projects that eventually led to these wins. I personally worked with the consortium team for six months before the Request for Tender came out, and at the time of the bid had been working with ACSO's business development team for almost a year.

In contrast, during the same period, I was asked to work with a business that delivered programmed maintenance services on another retention bid for an important contract. This time, we started work just as the Request for Tender was released. In the bid strategy workshop, it quickly became obvious that there were many problems with contract performance. The customer's tone and manner when corresponding with us during the Request for Tender period was abrupt and uncooperative. Although we worked hard, we were just too far behind to win again.

If only one thing stays with you when you reach the end of this book, I hope it's this – nothing is more important than starting early enough if you want to win again.

Planning creates projects. Through projects, we create positioning. Positioning creates clear winners.

Essentially, planning is just a way of getting all of your business-winning ideas out of your head and figuring out how you're going to achieve them. Planning gives you something to focus on, other than doing a great job and waiting for the Request for Tender. It gives you time to share with the customer everything you're doing, before the probity period locks down all communication. It also helps you to take a big chunk of your power back.

Actor Ray Liotta once said: "As soon as I started producing my own stuff, I started getting other roles." When you focus on your most important contracts and customers during business development planning, you create momentum that's compelling to other customers too.

The projects that result from planning help us to build something new and meaningful, not just to do more of what we are already doing today.

In his book *The New Rules of Management*, Peter Cook says the success in our lives comes down to the projects we implement. If you review your last 90 days at work and ask the question "how successful were they?" the answer will often be found in the new things you invested in, the ideas that helped you to do something better or differently.

In the next section of this book, Your Message, we're going to unpack exactly what it is you need to plan and develop into projects to give yourself the best chance of winning again.

This is your game plan to be ready to re-compete: to retain your most important contract or customer when they next decide to test the market. Throughout the rest of the book, it is referred to as your 'Ready to Re-compete Program'.

This program is a powerful way to position yourself with the customer as the obvious, and only, choice. It contains a series of projects – new ideas in development that demonstrate innovation, best practice and continual improvement – together with a plan for sustainable customer communication and engagement over the term of the contract.

The more ideas you create that are of value to customers, the better your business development results will be.

It's exciting and empowering work, so let's get on and do it.

Chapter summary – Getting Ready to Re-compete

☑   **Only about 50 per cent of incumbents will retain the business,** not because they're doing a poor job, but because they're still doing the same job.

☑   **Rollovers only happen at the buyer's option and discretion.** To regain control, think of your contract end date as an opportunity for renovation, redevelopment, and reinvigoration.

☑   **The opportunity gap exists between 'focus day-to-day' and 'improve day-to-day'.** Clear winners spend most of their time improving day-to-day, getting results that resonate in the customer's world and building the customer's future.

☑   **Transactional and therefore short-term suppliers think more like tenants,** taking the customer and the opportunity for granted.

☑   **Strategic, long-term suppliers think more like custodians,** recognising that their role is to add to the customer's business and to improve in some way.

☑   **Selling to procurement might look like it's all about paperwork, but actually it's all about positioning.** Planning creates positioning and helps you to take some of your power back.

PART 2

Your Message

To close the opportunity gap means to use your incumbency to your advantage, continually developing new ideas and better ways of doing things, and presenting these initiatives to your customer as often as possible. In this section, we explore the four main sources of sustainable competitive advantage for incumbent suppliers and hear how others leverage their incumbency advantage to retain their most important contracts and customers.

CHAPTER 3

Innovation

WE'VE EXAMINED THE IDEA that there are three sources of competitive advantage for incumbent suppliers:

- You **know more** than anybody else about the customer and their problems.

- You can **learn more** about their issues, because you can reach their decision makers in a way that competitors can't.

- This means you can **influence more** than others in your market, helping the customer to operate better, compete better or do business better.

These advantages are yours right now, and now is the time to seize them. If you wait too long, the competition cycle will roll around again and you will simply be compared to the market along with everyone else.

Procurement expert Adel Salman says: "Suppliers need to put forward a solution that actually addresses what we are becoming, not what we were in the past when you initially secured the business. In service contracts in particular, suppliers need to be very skilled at influencing the client – not in a manipulative way, but in an informative, educational way."

Today's risk-averse business culture can stifle innovation and make it difficult to come up with new ideas. This is especially true when it comes to anything that affects important contracts and customers. No matter how creative you were when you pitched for the contract, fear and self-preservation often take over when you are the incumbent.

However, as we saw earlier, you're the expert and the customer expects you to be able to build a picture of how their future might look if they continue to work with you. Bidding to provide services is never going to be completely transactional and all about price. It is always about something more. Buyers need help to navigate complex problems that weren't conceived of a year ago – let alone 10 years ago. New solutions can come from anywhere.

So let's talk about innovation and how it can help you create a sustainable competitive advantage to retain your most important contracts and customers.

What is all the fuss about innovation?

Innovation is a bit of a buzzword in business these days and you can't go five minutes on the Internet without seeing yet another commentator extolling the virtues of innovation.

Innovation is big business, and many business books published today talk about innovation. A current Amazon book search on the topic of innovation turns up more than 38000 titles.

But it's not enough to be interested in innovation just because it's topical.

A better reason to be interested in innovation is that your customers are. A quick review of the annual reports of Australia's top ten public companies shows that every single one of them has innovation, in some form, as one of their key strategic goals. Here are just a few examples.

- **Commonwealth Bank** says achieving and maintaining a leadership position in technology and innovation is a strategic and operational priority. CommBank just completed a five-year Core Banking Modernisation program in which it was the first major Australian bank to offer real-time settlement and real-time banking. Recent innovations include CommBank Kaching for Facebook, Australia's first social media banking application; Smartsign, a service allowing customers to execute loan documents electronically from anywhere in the world; and MyWealth, an online platform for self-directed investors.

- **Woodwide Petroleum** says it is seeking growth through exploration and innovation, expanding its global portfolio into deepwater sites in New Zealand and Ireland. Woodside is actively pursuing innovation in subsea development, which could substantially reduce costs for its major liquid natural gas projects. It also has external partnerships with research bodies and universities to extend its business capabilities and technological skills.

- **Wesfarmers** reports that it is working to develop a culture that encourages innovation and rewards boldness and creativity. One of its strategies is external benchmarking to ensure best practice and innovation that satisfies customer needs.

Does it surprise you to learn that the public sector is just as interested in innovation? According to the Grattan Institute, Australian governments spend more than $10 billion each year supporting innovation through research in the public sector, projects conducted through private firms, and tax credits for research and development.

The Australian federal government also promotes its public sector Innovation Toolkit, a website that gives practical advice on fostering innovation within public sector agencies.

Pretty much everyone is interested in innovation, and procurement is no exception.

A survey of 70 chief executive officers (CEOs) by brain.net revealed that CEOs expect much more from procurement departments in areas like innovation. As customers improve their procurement processes and take a different view of suppliers, innovating together becomes part of doing business. In his book *Selling To Procurement*, Christopher Provines says:

> "Increasingly, particularly for more mature organisations, procurement is being asked to help the company grow. The average business has thousands of suppliers, all with a full range of capabilities, expertise and ideas. Smart companies have begun to look at the supply base more strategically ... as a potential source of innovation and growth. Innovation needs to be thought of in the broadest sense – process/ business model innovation and product innovation. Often, suppliers can contribute significantly to both."

Provines cites a survey of more than 300 chief purchasing officers by CAPS Research, a supply chain research firm, which revealed that about 60 per cent saw innovation from suppliers as "extremely important". For example, Proctor & Gamble's outward-focused approach to innovation, called Connect and Develop, resulted in 40 per cent of new product innovations originating outside the company.

This is encouraging news for suppliers, and here is even more.

Service providers and procurement are actually natural allies, according to procurement expert Adel Salman.

"Unlike suppliers of raw materials, procurement doesn't own the [expenditure] and has to satisfy many other stakeholders who are actually using the service and paying for it," Salman explains. Therefore, it's in procurement's interests to invest time in service providers like you, and work with you to deliver exceptional service performance.

"By working with procurement, you will more likely deliver the type of services required across the business," Salman says. "There's a mutual objective there."

And it all starts with innovation. So what does innovation mean for you, and how can you build innovation into your Ready to Re-compete Program to retain your most important contracts and customers?

Customers want you to help them to build their future.

When you're selling complex services through long term contracts, it's what you're striving for that's important, not where you are right now. The client is buying you as you are today, but also where you will be in three years' time. 'Business as usual' may be comfortable, but it's also a trap you don't want to fall into.

If you have just signed a contract with a new customer, now is the ideal time to start building an innovation plan.

Innovation is fascinating and inspiring, but it's also time consuming and difficult. New projects take time to deliver results and give us tangible evidence to talk to the customer about.

Even if your contract is well underway, start thinking about innovation now, as early as you can, to give yourself the best chance when you need to re-compete.

Procurement expert Neil Hubbard supports this concept wholeheartedly.

"Don't wait until it's time to do a tender," says Hubbard. "As soon as you're awarded the contract, your time starts. Be very conscious that in three years' time, your contract will come up. Start working on innovation that will bring cost savings or benefits to our business and start telling us what you're going to do now."

Innovating with the customer in mind is different to innovating for yourself.

Think of yourself as a 'tastemaker' – an expert who popularises something new.

When you are a tastemaker, you know what your client wants before they do.

It's like taking a friend to your favourite restaurant and guiding them through the menu. To do this in a way that delivers a good experience for both of you requires consideration of their preferences and compassion for their point of view, coupled with the conviction that your expertise will guide them towards the best result.

Tastemakers become famous for their innovations, for their ability to bring us something revolutionary that changes the way we live, work or relate to one another. Facebook's Mark Zuckerberg is a tastemaker. Vogue's Anna Wintour is a tastemaker. The late Steve Jobs from Apple was a tastemaker.

Mark Zuckerberg's innovation, Facebook, has fundamentally changed the way we communicate and connect. We may take it for granted now, but being able to share important life events with the people closest to us with a single click of the mouse or swipe of the finger is unprecedented in history. Facebook has operated for more than a decade, and now has at least a billion users, which means it's easier to find people than ever before. One woman who had been searching for her birth mother for many years took only two days to find her via Facebook.

Anna Wintour is a tastemaker in the $160 billion global fashion industry. Wintour has been editor-in-chief at Vogue since 1988 – a freakishly long time in magazine years. She not only has an enormous impact on what people choose to wear, but also her innovations have transformed the way the fashion industry does business. Wintour is credited with the end of the supermodel era, as the first to put celebrities rather than models on magazine covers. She built the careers of globally recognised designers including Marc Jacobs and Alexander McQueen. Wintour has long been an advocate of the 'democratisation' of fashion:

making aspirational fashion accessible to everyone. One of the first things Wintour did as editor-in-chief at Vogue in 1988 was to put a model on the cover in a pair of $50 jeans and a $10,000 jewel-encrusted T-shirt. This started fashion designers thinking about how to get their work in front of more people, and now, many world-famous designers – including Stella McCartney, Isaac Mizrahi and Karl Lagerfeld – have collaborated with high-street retailers such as H&M and Target.

Hundreds of thousands of words have already been written about the impact and legacy of Steve Jobs, who revolutionised the computing, entertainment, music and telecommunications industries. Where would we be without the iPod, iPad and iPhone?

Each of these tastemakers has had a movie made specifically about them: *The Social Network* (Zuckerberg), *September Issue* (Wintour) and *Jobs* (Steve Jobs). Each has been the inspiration for countless followers in art and in business.

So where can you find your inspiration?

Go wide for new ideas

Competitive advantage means taking risks and moving away from what we know, something that is neither comfortable nor easy to do. It doesn't mean doing exactly what everybody else is doing.

Have you ever seen movies where the hero swings across an impossible impasse, runs up the side of a building, or does a backflip off a dumpster? Then you've witnessed parkour, an intensely physical sport where adventurous types get from A to B using only their bodies and their surroundings to propel themselves.

Parkour practitioners work solo, not in teams, and to avoid injury they must look at their environment in ways that most of us can't even imagine.

When it comes to scanning our competitive landscape, most of us could learn a lot from parkour practitioners. We tend to see our markets as a familiar track we have run around many times before, rather than as an exciting playground full of new things to try.

The other day I was walking around my neighbourhood when I saw something surprising – three identical 18-month-olds sitting on a tricycle built specifically for triplets. What a great idea.

Our customers' businesses are full of opportunities like this; things they need built to solve problems they deal with every day, in this case how to manage three toddlers who all want to get on a bike at the same time.

If you're pitching for a multimillion dollar contract, you will be in a competition of equals who can probably do the job just as well as you can. Often, it's the very small things that will tip the buyer over the edge to choose a winner.

In a highly regulated market where competitive advantage is hard to come by, it's surprising to overlook one when it presents itself. Yet that's exactly what recently happened in professional football here in Australia.

Professional football is big business, and all clubs are looking for an edge to win a premiership flag. Finding one is by no means easy.

While the professional league was recently contending with salary caps and supplements scandals, former high school physical education teacher Peta Searle was busy working as an assistant coach at Port Melbourne in the amateur league. Searle built the competition's best defence back line at Port Melbourne, and helped the club to win a premiership. Unfortunately, Searle was paid very little in the amateur league and needed a job in the professional leagues to make a decent living. Despite her outstanding track record, she couldn't get one.

From a purely commercial standpoint, this made no sense at all. Searle was a proven performer. If she had been born a man, her achievements probably would have started a bidding war. After the national media raised her profile, eventually the St Kilda football club recognised that Searle could be their competitive advantage and recruited her as the AFL's first female development coach.

Breakthrough thinking and insights come not only from thinking more laterally about what's right in front of our noses, but from educating ourselves in ideas and disciplines that are outside our core area of expertise, our industry, or our life experience. We can learn leadership from an explorer who has spent time leading a team in Antarctica, or learn better ways to relate to colleagues and customers by talking to a social worker who helps people navigate very complex personal or family issues.

It's best to think more broadly about professional development than simply focusing on technical training that further entrenches the status quo. Technical training is an important way to keep staff qualifications up-to-date, but mostly maintains the baseline and isn't the best way to deliver new thinking – especially when all your competitors are doing the same programs.

One of the ways Steve Jobs came up with new ideas was to maintain a lifelong interest in learning and new experiences. While in college, Jobs took a course in calligraphy, which at the time had no practical application to his work. What he experienced came to life later in the Macintosh computer, the first of its kind to prioritise typeface, fonts and calligraphy.

Good ideas don't have to be radical to be effective.

Innovation means 'new and improved', but there's no hard and fast way of defining what can be classed as an innovation.

Innovation can be evolutionary (make incremental improvements) or revolutionary (make ground-breaking improvements). Both are valuable and neither should be discounted in the search for innovations that will resonate with a customer.

Neil Hubbard experienced both evolutionary and revolutionary innovation from suppliers while he worked at Crown Casino in Melbourne.

Crown Casino is a huge complex that occupies 510,000 square metres – the equivalent of two city blocks – on the banks of the Yarra River in Melbourne. Crown is visited by as many as 16 million people each year, more than 50,000 per day and up to

120,000 during major sporting events. More than 80,000 cars enter the car park each week.

Maintaining the facility is a massive job. Painting Crown Casino is a bit like painting the Sydney Harbour Bridge, where the crew finishes one end and goes back to the other to start again.

Hubbard asked the incumbent painting supplier whether there was a way to do things better and differently. Apparently there was.

The painting supplier told Hubbard about a new paint now available on the market. It was thicker, adhered better and was more resistant, so it didn't chip when you knocked it. It was good for high-traffic areas and the painters wouldn't have so much work to do.

Hubbard asked why the supplier hadn't already shared the idea. The supplier replied that nobody had asked him, and he didn't think Crown would be interested because the agreement required his team to simply come in and paint. Hubbard asked if it would cost more to move to the new type of paint: it would, but the labour cost would drop. And because the painter didn't need to supply so much labour, he was free to pick up work elsewhere. Both Crown and the painting company were better off as a result.

This is a great example of an **evolutionary improvement** that delivered benefits both to the customer and to the supplier. And aside from the way it changed the nature of the painting contract, Crown didn't need to rope off its facilities for painting quite as often, reducing inconvenience for casino patrons and providing a better atmosphere.

Hubbard also recalls a time when an enterprising new supplier pointed out a problem Crown didn't even realise it had: people leaving the venue because their mobile phone had gone flat and needed recharging.

The proposed solution was a self-charging unit that Crown could mount on its walls. It would not only keep customers entertained at Crown for longer, but also make Crown a destination for those in the area who needed to charge their phone.

This was such a good idea that Hubbard and his team didn't even look to the market for other options. "We ran a trial for three months and saw that this actually brought people to Crown and ... they stayed on the site. Now, portable phone charging sites can be seen everywhere, but at the time this just worked really well for us. It was an idea that a supplier brought to us that hadn't even come onto our radar yet," Hubbard explains.

This is an example of a **revolutionary improvement** from a new or prospective supplier, but the principles remain the same if you're an incumbent supplier. In fact, you are in a better position than anybody else to see the issues that your customer faces every day, and think about interesting new ways to resolve them.

For a customer to buy innovation, it must be meaningful

Meaningful innovation resonates with the customer's goals. The most meaningful innovations also solve one or more of the customer's big, gnarly problems – preferably problems that no one else has been able to solve yet. Innovations that focus on opportunity creation can also be useful, but are harder to sell, unless you have a growth-minded customer and the potential of a big payoff or return.

The father of psychoanalysis, Sigmund Freud, suggests: "We will do more to avoid pain than to gain pleasure."

Much of the time, customers are more motivated to buy something that solves a big gnarly problem than they are to recognise an opportunity. We are much more motivated to resolve an issue that is keeping us up at night than we are to take a risk on a bright shiny opportunity that may or may not be better than our current reality.

For example, my family gave up its old 'fatback' television only a month before the analogue signal in our area was switched off forever. We had bought a set-top box so we could watch digital television channels, but the box didn't receive the digital signal very well, so we never used it and just kept watching the old analogue channels.

When we moved house, we took the TV with us to our new (two storey) place, where it was installed upstairs. It weighed 60 kilograms. Not long after we moved, we realised the analogue signal was about to go off forever, rendering the TV useless. So we actually had to hire the removalists back to take it down the stairs and take it away!

As it turned out, my family wasn't really that interested in buying a new TV to watch all the extra channels offered by digital TV (the bright shiny opportunity). We didn't change over our old TV set until we were faced with the prospect of a black screen (big gnarly problem).

So before we get too excited about what we want to offer that might be innovative, it is important to think about the customer's goals, pressing problems and their appetite for change. For example, NAB's Tehara Wickham says the bank has high expectations of a supplier's offer in the areas of environmental sustainability and innovation, and particularly so when it comes to incumbent suppliers, as these are both issues that are particularly important to them.

Innovation means understanding customer problems and packaging solutions

Have you ever lost to a competitor who offered something different to what the customer was asking for? Then you lost to a competitor who was better at innovation.

Lateral thinking guru Edward De Bono says: "One very important aspect of innovation is the willingness to stop and to look at things that no one else has bothered to look at. This simple process of focusing on things that are normally taken for granted is a powerful source of creativity."

Conformity no longer works in business, says Seth Godin in his book *Purple Cow*, and it's all about creating remarkable products and services that the right customers actively seek out. "Instead of trying to use your technology and expertise to make a better product or service for the way your customers do things today, think of ways that your service could work better if users would change their behaviour, even if only slightly," Godin suggests.

This is exactly what your competitors will be doing. Challengers know that they need to disrupt the status quo, and offer something radically better than what you are offering in an effort to encourage the customer to change suppliers.

As the incumbent, you may have an interest in retaining the status quo, but your status quo should feel more like a flight of stairs you are climbing than a flat and comfortable pathway.

ACSO CEO Karenza Louis-Smith learned a valuable lesson about the value of innovation and stepping up from the status quo when she and her consortium partners lost an employment services bid to a competitor several years ago. The delivery of government employment services to job seekers is a sizeable market and many providers deliver a very similar offer. What she heard in the debriefing session with the Department of Employment changed the way she approached the packaging and promotion of her organisation's ideas.

"The organisation they chose was doing everything the same as us, but they badged and floated an innovation around 11 different flavours of coffee in their employment services suites. At the time I was thinking, 'What are they talking about, eleven flavours of coffee? Who gives a *#(@$*about the flavours of coffee?'" Karenza said.

Of course, it wasn't really about the coffee at all. The customer bought the idea of job seeker engagement – how to get jobseekers and employers connected. "These coffee lounges had employer guest breakfasts and a whole bunch of things in them, and it was a different, exciting way of doing things. It was creative, it was thought provoking and it was a way to get a better outcome. [The other organisation] had a vision about what they were going to do and how they were going to do it, and it was packaged and sold in such a way that it was exciting. I learned a lot from that experience," Karenza says.

In this case, the big gnarly problem was how to normalise the process of accessing government employment services, both for jobseekers and employers, and get them comfortable interacting with one another.

Start with the customer's problems, and look for interesting ways to solve them.

Innovation is not a one-time thing – it's an 'all the time' thing

Individuals and teams that keep thinking and innovating are always going to win more business than those that don't. So innovation is not just about the systems, products and services you build, it's actually about having a process for continuing to generate improvement ideas.

There are formal, organisational innovation processes like the Ten Types of Innovation, and then there are things that we can each do individually to improve our ability to innovate.

Harvard Business School identifies the four key ingredients for continuous innovation by individuals as domain expertise; the ability to learn new things; creative thinking; and working hard. Domain expertise is about a depth of knowledge and skill in the area you work in. This is something you already have in spades. Being able to learn new things – both inside and outside your comfort zone – will help with creative thinking and original ideas. Hard work speaks for itself.

To me, this sounds like a pretty good recipe for career success. When innovation becomes a habit, you win, the team wins and so does the customer.

Innovation needs to be resourced properly in order to be successful

By now we've established that innovation is important, but like a lot of things that sound great in theory, it's much harder to do in practice.

The three elements that need to be present for successful innovation are ideas, time and the ability to invest. These resources exist in varying degrees at any point in time and also vary depending on the size of the organisation.

- Small organisations generally have ideas and time, but lack the ability to make a significant financial investment. Partnerships can work well here. Karenza Louis-Smith recalls a time she worked with a consortium looking to win a services contract with the Department of Justice. Their initial bid was unsuccessful, but they were encouraged to try again and each organisation invested a small amount of capital in a pilot project and contributed their best staff to run it. The pilot went well and the consortium won the business next time.

- Medium-sized organisations often find that they are so flat out delivering all of their commitments that there is no time to generate ideas, let alone see them come to fruition. Medium-sized organisations have often grown to this size on the strength of an initial innovation that has given them significant traction in a particular marketplace. While ability to invest in innovation isn't so much of a problem, making it a priority can be. I've seen medium-sized organisations win contracts only to lose them three years later, due to lack of new ideas. Taking one step forward and one step backwards in this way can be extremely frustrating when you want to achieve sustainable growth.

- In large organisations, the situation changes again. Large organisations are full of smart people with good ideas, and if they choose to they can find the time to be innovative and get the financial backing to see their ideas come to life. However, the issue here becomes one of organisational fit. When organisations get to a certain size, they have a fairly fixed idea of who they are and what they are about, and it is harder to give people the freedom to pursue innovations that do not conform. So a breakaway from the mother ship can be a good way for large organisations to invest in innovation. Technology giant Google has invested in Google Campus, an environment that encourages innovation for technology start-ups through collaboration, mentorship and networking. Google Campus operates in London, Tel Aviv and Warsaw, and provides tech innovators with mentoring and training from Google employees and experienced entrepreneurs.

No matter what size they are, the most successful suppliers firmly embed innovation in their culture, and it's not something that people are expected to undertake on top of their busy day job. Tim Ferriss, author of the *Four-Hour Work Week*, says that 88 per cent of employees have a hard time juggling work and life, 53 per cent would opt for a personal assistant rather than personal trainer and 34 per cent report difficulty in sleeping due to work-related stress. Expecting individuals to set aside specific time for innovation can be unrealistic, unless it is part of their actual job role or deliverables.

For example, engineering firm Arup truly values innovation. It has a strong focus on design, and the people who are drawn to work there are encouraged to spend their time pursuing new and better ways of doing things. "It's almost like breathing – innovation is just something everyone does here," says Arup's Catherine Redden.

Some years ago I worked on a bid for an organisation that manufactured hearing aids. Its products were considered the Bang & Olufsen of hearing aids, some of the best-designed and most advanced products in the world. The local Australian office was bidding for a federal government tender and our bid control centre, more commonly known as a 'war room', was located in one of the internal meeting rooms. One day I noticed that the managing director had pasted a new sign on our war room door. The sign said 'Skunkworks'.

A 'skunkworks' is a project developed by a small and loosely structured group of people primarily for the sake of radical innovation. Skunkworks is also the official alias for defence powerhouse Lockheed Martin's advanced development programs. Lockheed's skunkworks project in World War II designed a number of new aircraft. Today, the term skunkworks is used in business, engineering and technical fields to describe a group of people who are given a high degree of autonomy and are tasked with working on advanced or secret projects.

Consider how you and your team can think of your Ready to Re-compete Program as a kind of skunkworks – an advanced and ambitious program that remains unhampered by bureaucracy.

Chapter summary – Innovation

☑ **Seize the day.** Don't wait until the competition cycle rolls around again, or you will be compared to the market like everyone else.

☑ **Procurement and service providers are natural allies.** Procurement answers to the business for the quality of services you deliver. It's in their interests to work with you and help you succeed.

☑ **You are the tastemaker, and your job is to know what your client wants before they do.** Use Mark Zuckerberg, Anna Wintour or Steve Jobs as inspiration.

☑ **We want our big, gnarly problems to be resolved.** Suppliers who work to solve the customer's problems will get more appreciation than those that don't.

☑ **Innovation can be evolutionary or revolutionary.** Both types are valuable to customers.

☑ **Buyers need help to navigate complex problems,** and suppliers who keep thinking and keep innovating are always going to win more business.

☑ **Innovation requires ideas, time and investment to be successful.** If you're small, find a way to invest. If you're medium-sized, make innovation a priority even while you are knee-deep in delivery. And if you're large, adjust your culture or create a skunkworks to make it ok for people to pursue ideas that may not conform.

CHAPTER 4

Best Practice

WHEN WE CONSIDER SOURCES of competitive advantage, we mostly think about what we can create that is uniquely our own and sets us apart from competitors (innovations), and things we can do to improve what we are already doing (operational excellence and continual improvement).

Both are important.

And then there's another source of sustainable competitive advantage that few suppliers are leveraging as well as they could be. Best practice.

When a customer buys from us, it's important to remember that they are sacrificing other options. And they expect that they are getting the best solution in the market.

Best practice represents the highest level of performance achieved in the industry as a whole, rather than by a single supplier, and best practices are techniques that have consistently shown results that are better than those achieved by other methods. Some examples include industry standards and benchmarks where there is quantitative evidence, and 'leading practices' where evidence is mostly qualitative or it is difficult to identify a standard or benchmark.

It's not always all about us and our ideas, and there is almost always more that we can do to convince the customer that we are looking as widely as possible to deliver the best results for them.

Building best practice means looking further afield in ways that will stretch our thinking, build value and cement an unassailable competitive position when it's time for the customer to compare us to the wider market.

So how can best practice help you to build value into your offer, and retain your most important contracts and customers?

If innovation makes you the artist, best practice makes you the art gallery curator.

You are turning your expert eye to what is happening in the industry, and collecting the pieces that will most appeal to your customer's tastes and needs.

'Content curation' is a term that has gained currency in recent years amongst bloggers and online marketers. At its most basic, this type of curation means finding, and judiciously sharing, information that will be of interest to an online audience.

In an interview with Fastcompany.com, content strategist Erin Scime defined content curation as "knowing your collection as a subject matter expert to very fine detail ... figuring out how to communicate and educate people on what is there and how they can find it, and reaching out to a larger community."

Scime explains that when a website launches and an audience starts to show up interested in learning more, it's critical to establish what the website owner knows most about. This helps to assert the brand's authority, establishes relationships with its audience, and secures a return visit based on the value of the content the brand is sharing.

In this case, the brand is you and your team, and the way you deliver the contract.

The channel is not a public one, like a website, but a professional one.

There are many rich sources of best practice you can tap into – all you need to do is start looking.

Sources of best practice

The first source of best practice is **our own business**: what we are doing for other customers that we may not yet be offering this one.

The second is **competitors**: the best of what's on offer from direct competitors in our market.

The third source of best practice is **others**: either in allied or non-allied industries that share similar customers, tackle the same issues or have similar operational needs.

The value created when we look both at our own business and at competitors' businesses is that we can **leverage current practices** to get the best possible outcome for the customer.

The value created when we look more widely, at competitors and others, is that we **learn from successful partnerships** and find out what the wider market is doing to achieve good results.

Finally, the value created when we draw parallels between our own business and what others are doing is that we are able to **link similar problems**. Where can we learn from others, or partner with them to achieve a win for us, for them and for our customer?

Figure 2: Three sources of best practice that help clear winners to link, leverage and learn from what's already out there, and bring the best of the market to the customer.

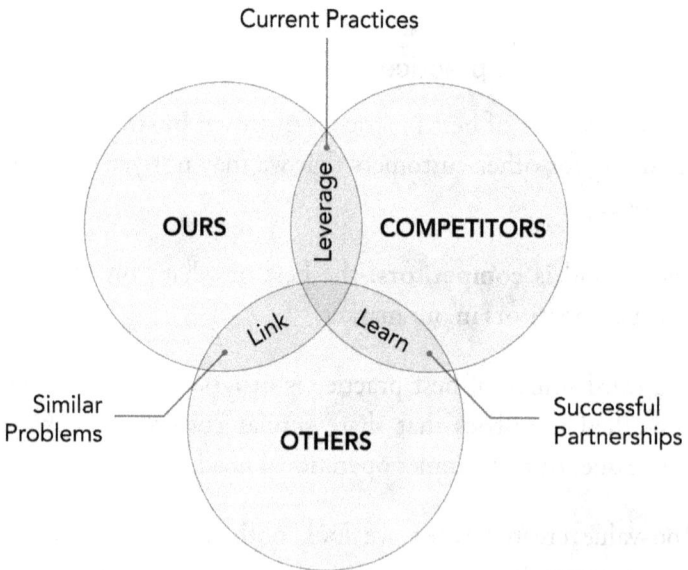

Looking in our own backyard

Working with a large and demanding customer can stretch and challenge an organisation's service delivery practices. As we know, the first source of best practice is our own business – what we're doing for other customers that we may not yet be offering to this one.

Every Statement of Requirement and commercial contract is subtly different, and you will often find that there are practices your organisation has developed elsewhere for other customers that could work for your important customer too.

Talk to the people who manage other key accounts. You might be surprised at what you learn, and pick up great ideas you can apply straight away.

For example, I worked with a large consulting services firm on a retention pitch for one of their largest customers, one of Australia's major banks. The service they provided was tailored to the bank's staff members, and geographically complex. The bank was considering renewing the firm's contract, but needed a bit of a push to make the final decision. We knew that to convince them to sign on for a longer contract, we needed to prove they were getting the best service in the market from the strongest operational provider.

We found that they weren't even getting best practice from within their own business: another team managing the account for a large resources company had developed a suite of exceptional offerings for this large, geographically complex and demanding customer. We sat down with the resources team, compared their service delivery model with ours and devised several quick wins and a handful of other improvements that could be implemented if the contract was renegotiated. So before we even started looking elsewhere, we found a number of ways to offer the bank the benefit of our experience with another major customer, which gave a huge boost to the retention effort.

Looking to competitors

Unpalatable as this sounds, the innovations you're developing probably will not hold your market space forever.

All new things become old eventually. As soon as an innovation is mature, it becomes best practice because it resets the customer's baseline expectation. Depending on your market, you may only have weeks, months or years to capitalise on your innovation.

The exposure that designers get at prestigious Fashion Week shows around the globe has had some unintended consequences. Now, fashion knockoff designers can replicate high-end designs and sell them into high street outlets months before they hit the luxury brand stores. This is exasperating to luxury brand designers, and has apparently caused many to rethink whether they should actually be showing at Fashion Weeks.

And this is not a particularly new phenomenon. Remember Palm Pilots? I had one of those. Palm Pilots, Pocket PCs and Blackberries were the first wave of smart phones. Some of these were available as early as the turn of the century (which makes them sound as old as they seem to us now). These early smart phones were an innovation that dramatically reduced the mass market for paper diaries.

The iPhone launched in 2007 and revolutionised the way we organised our lives. Similar Android smartphones started appearing in 2008, and two years later they were everywhere, but

Apple's iPhone innovation still dominated the mobile market for around five years (a very long time in tech years).Then things changed again. By the end of 2013, Samsung accounted for 32.3 per cent of all smartphone sales, while Apple came in second with 15.5 per cent. Samsung was now selling twice as many smartphones as Apple.

In technology, you can be known as a fast innovator or a fast follower. In business, you probably want to do both. Look at what competitors are offering, and figure out how you can offer something similar. If you don't, your competitors surely will.

I was once asked to lead a resurrection effort with a supplier that had lost its biggest and longest-standing customer. The supplier delivered brochures, flyers and other marketing communications material, and had built its service delivery model when volumes were much lower. Unfortunately, the enquiry hotline for non-deliveries was managed by the customer rather than by the supplier and over the years, a growing number of calls to the hotline reinforced the perception that the supplier was not controlling the rise in non-deliveries. The competitor, on the other hand, offered to manage the hotline itself, which achieved two things. It removed the perception problem (there are always non-deliveries in this type of business) and gave the impression of a better customer service system.

Looking further afield and making valuable connections

Another source of best practice can be found in allied or non-allied industries that share similar customers, tackle the same issues, or have similar operational needs. How can we learn from others, or partner with them, to achieve a win for us, for them and for our customer?

An excellent example of this approach can be found in a partnership between three entities that share overlapping interests. One is a business, another is a not-for-profit organisation and the final partner is a government department.

The Step UP Loan Program is a partnership between National Australia Bank (NAB), Good Shepherd Microfinance and the federal government's Department of Social Services (DSS), formerly the Department of Families, Housing, Community Services and Indigenous Affairs (FaHCSIA).

It helps vulnerable, low-income people who can't afford essential items that most of us take for granted – including fridges and washing machines. At time of writing, the Step UP program offered loans worth up to $3000 repayable over three years at an interest rate of 3.99 per cent.

NAB and Good Shepherd Micro-Finance have a common interest in lending. This two-handed partnership was enough to launch the StepUP Loans initiative into Victoria and New South Wales in 2004.

Good Shepherd Micro-Finance and DSS have in common an interest in alleviating the effects of poverty. DSS joined the program to support its growth in 2010, and Step UP loans are now offered nationally.

Financial inclusion is a common interest for NAB and DSS. NAB has an active corporate social responsibility program and measures the impact of these programs through a Social Return on Investment methodology. DSS is responsible for providing services to vulnerable people in the community.

Step UP Loans offer an alternative to 'payday' lenders, which target vulnerable people who need money but are unable to access credit. Payday loans often charge interest rates as high as 1000 per cent.

A study by The Centre for Social Impact showed that the Step UP program is improving financial inclusion for many vulnerable people, with 64.6 per cent of loan clients no longer borrowing from fringe lenders and 73.6 per cent experiencing a 'net positive change' in economic and social outcomes like financial literacy, confidence, social and health outcomes. The Step UP Loan was awarded *Money Magazine*'s Best Socially Responsible Product in 2007, 2008 and 2009.

You could create a similar initiative for your industry – it just takes a good idea and the right connections to get it started. There might be a problem that both you and your customer are keen to solve, and a third party could help make it happen. Take the initiative to broker a relationship and bring the third party to the table.

Another potential source of ideas for best practice comes from 'centres of excellence'.

In industry terms, a centre of excellence is a group of people that come together with their organisation's backing to share best practices in a particular area of expertise.

A quick Google search, typing 'centre of excellence' and the name of your industry will reveal what is already out there and available for you to learn from. A search for the engineering industry showed up the Engineering Centre of Excellence, Centre for Future Energy Networks, Military Engineering

Centre of Excellence and Centre of Excellence in Farm Machinery Condition Monitoring, to name just a few. There is probably already a group in existence for your topic of interest. Some will be academic networks, while others are coalitions of organisations in the same arena. These groups may be local, national or international.

The greatest leverage comes from being involved in groups that do not compete within the same market boundary. In this environment, people feel more comfortable sharing ideas and learning from one another. Some of my most successful clients have used these relationships to arrange reciprocal study tours, conference speaking opportunities and staff secondments. There is an inspiring world out there, and a lot to learn from others' achievements.

Chapter summary – Best Practice

☑ **Best practice is an important source of competitive advantage.** When a customer buys from us, they sacrifice other options. Make sure they are getting the best solution in the market.

☑ **Look in your own backyard.** Find out what your organisation is doing for other customers, and share these best practices with your customer.

☑ **Gauge market expectations.** When an innovation is mature it becomes a best practice, because it resets the customer's baseline expectations.

☑ **Be a fast innovator and a fast follower.** Look at what competitors are offering, and figure out how you can offer something similar.

☑ **Find new partners you can bring to the relationship** who are interested in helping you and the customer solve a mutual problem, or create a mutual opportunity.

☑ **Join centres of excellence in your field, or create your own.** Find a group that is committed to sharing best practices, and contribute generously.

☑ **Leverage your best practice connections** as a source of learning and staff development as well as new ideas to bring to your contract or customer.

CHAPTER 5

Operational Excellence and Continual Improvement

CUSTOMERS EXPECT OPERATIONAL EXCELLENCE. They also expect that you will continually improve the work you deliver day to day.

Operational excellence means doing what you are paid to do and doing it exceptionally well. This is a contractual expectation, and paying attention to operational excellence should happen naturally.

Now that every organisation managing large contracts is quality accredited, or has a quality program, there is also an expectation that you will regularly improve what you deliver. Continual improvement is a central requirement of quality management, and is something you will be assessed on when you're audited to keep your quality accreditation. Getting in front of customers with better ways of doing business should therefore also be a routine part of what you do.

Each procurement expert I spoke to for this book shared his or her frustration that most suppliers don't suggest ideas for continual improvement as often as they should.

Tehara Wickham, Head of Procurement Governance and Engagement at National Australia Bank, oversees procurement across NAB's entire business, and sees this problem on wide scale.

"When we go into a tender, we have existing suppliers who talk about all of the new fancy [things] that they could be doing for us, "Wickham says.

"And as a customer, there's always this question of, 'Well, why aren't you already doing that?' We've had a five-year contract or a ten-year contract. Things move and change. You get the feeling that people have been keeping stuff in their back pocket to offer up at tender time, as opposed to coming to us as a valued customer during the original contract."

Wickham is aware that it isn't always easy to make changes within a contract term, but it's important to try when you're talking about improvements that could benefit both parties. If you feel as though your ideas are not cutting through with the people you contact regularly, go wider and higher. Otherwise, there is a risk that you will find yourself in front of the procurement manager at the end of your contract, being asked why you haven't already brought these ideas to their attention.

First things first – do what you are paid to do consistently and well

Doing a good job is important, and when you first won the business you put in place everything you needed to deliver the work and deliver it well. Things change over time, and we need to be mindful of the 'recency effect', which tells us that the most recently presented items or experiences will most likely be remembered best.

If you've ever walked into a customer's office expecting a routine conversation, and spent the whole meeting talking about last week's non-delivery or someone's stuff-up yesterday, you'll know exactly what I mean.

Humans have pretty selective memories. We judge much of our life experience not on the totality, the average, or a glance back over the highlights, but on the basis of the last few minutes.

In *Change Anything,* a *New York Times* bestseller about the science of personal success, the authors conclude that much of what we feel about our daily relationships stems from only a few moments that overwhelmingly colour our perception.

Change Anything relates a study by Nobel laureate Daniel Kahneman, who asked colonoscopy patients to rate their level of discomfort during an unanaesthetised procedure. The results were surprising. An individual's comfort rating had almost nothing to do with the total amount of pain that they felt during the awkward and uncomfortable process. The only thing that mattered was how painful it was right at the end.

In the first study, Kahneman didn't control how long the colonoscopy took but asked people to rate their pain every 60 seconds. The duration of the procedure didn't predict the memory of pain: instead, pain was predicted by the most pain felt and the amount of pain felt in the final few minutes. In the second study, Kahneman had the doctor leave the probe in without moving it for the last 60 seconds. This recency manipulation had a huge impact on the patient's memory of pain. When the procedure ended well, patients recalled the experience as far less unpleasant.

While it might seem a little strange to compare colonoscopies with contract delivery, for a customer giving over control of part of their business to a supplier, it can feel like being operated on without an anaesthetic.

However well you're doing, it's important to ramp up your vigilance over day-to-day delivery at least three months before you need to compete again, so that your good work doesn't get derailed by one or two mistakes.

The Department of Foreign Affairs and Trade issues travel warnings to Australians planning to travel overseas. When things are going well in a particular country, the advice is to 'exercise normal safety precautions'. When there is an issue or some form of unrest, the advice steps up to 'exercise a high degree of caution'.

As you get closer to your competition (re-tender) date, exercise a high degree of caution so that the customer's lasting impression of you is a good one.

Continual improvement is a renovation project

In Chapter 3 we talked about innovation. We saw that innovation helps us to become 'tastemakers' – experts who popularise something new.

When we deliver something innovative, we often start from scratch – a bit like we do when we build a new home.

If innovation is like building a new home, continual improvement is more of a renovation project.

My grandmother's home was built in the 1940s with a kitchen upgrade in the 1970s. For most of my life, Nanna's house looked exactly the same. While this felt comfortable and familiar to me, to anyone outside the family, Nanna's place would have looked increasingly worn over time.

Likewise, a contract or customer relationship can start to look and feel like a time capsule. And we don't want to wait until it looks shabby to make improvements.

So how can we build continual improvement into the way we do things for the customer, in a way that not only meets expectations but surprises and delights them too?

Reporting on current performance

The first area to look at is current performance — what you are already doing well, where you need to improve and what you can do to overachieve.

Most service delivery contracts contain a service level agreement or series of key performance indicators (KPIs) that need to be met. Usually, the customer sets these KPIs and you agree to them when you take on the work. Sometimes there is an opportunity to set or negotiate your own.

As a provider of services, it's particularly important to quantify your value proposition and make it as tangible as you can. While you're deep in the delivery of a contract, this means thinking about how you can use reporting data to help the customer understand the value they are getting from you, and to enhance their opinion of your offer.

Ask yourself when you and your customer last reviewed your KPIs, as opposed to simply measuring them. Often, performance can be measured more accurately as delivery progresses, and there may be ways to adjust and enhance your KPIs so that they provide better information for both of you.

If you are serving end users on behalf of your customer, they will probably be interested in information about 'delivery in full and on time' rates, end-user complaints and dispute resolution times. If you are delivering projects, they will be interested in time, cost and quality measures.

NAB's Tehara Wickham talks about the need for true alignment between what the buyer thinks they are buying, and what the supplier thinks they are selling. Setting meaningful metrics for performance helps with this considerably. Delivering a consistent level of operational excellence further reassures the customer, gives them confidence and reduces any expectation that your work may cause them pain or discomfort.

A willingness to be transparent and critically evaluate your performance is also highly regarded by customers. Nothing is ever perfect. When things go wrong in the work or the relationship, as they inevitably will, the customer wants to know you're the kind of people they can work with to find a solution. "It's not fatal that there are issues in a contract; it's fatal not to address them," says procurement expert Adel Salman.

Think too about how easily the customer can access your performance data. Figure out ways to open up your systems and let people see what you are doing.

In an industry that mostly relies on relatively simple tracking of job completion and invoicing, Skybridge – which installs and maintains technical infrastructure – has taken field workforce management and reporting to a whole new level. As a result, the company now considers itself not just a contracting company, but also a workflow process specialist that invests heavily in continual improvement. Almost 20 per cent of Skybridge's employees are embedded in its systems development team.

Skybridge's technicians use its specially developed workflow apps systems on iPhones and iPads. The company also offers its customers real-time visibility of what's happening in the field, using password-protected portals that encourage the customer to reach deep inside their systems.

"This creates an unmatched level of integrity in terms of what we're doing, because we can't hide a mistake," Skybridge CEO Michael Abela says. Skybridge achieves a high level of performance in demanding, high volume contracts precisely because it fosters this type of transparency. And customers love the fact that they can login at any time to see what the Skybridge team is up to.

Once you've got current performance right, and recognising that this will change all the time, there are a couple of areas where you can look to find continual improvement ideas.

Let's talk then about contract delivery and service delivery.

Improving contract delivery

How can you better manage the contract so that it is efficient and effective both for you and for your customer?

A lot of administration and communication goes into major contracts and customer relationships. We've already talked about KPIs and service level agreements, but these are just the beginning.

Administration and communication are day-to-day activities that can potentially create friction and irritate a customer.

Do customers regularly call your organisation? Who do they speak to? How many emails a day do they see from you? Are they purely for information, or do they all require an answer? Do they interact with staff or field representatives? What kind of reporting and invoicing do they see? How often do they see them? What do they use the reports for? Do they log into your system to retrieve information? Any one or any combination of these could potentially irritate a customer.

It's important to understand all the ways the customer comes into contact with you and what their experience is at each point of contact. Once you have all the facts, you can open up an honest dialogue with your team about what needs to change.

You can also look at ways to improve value for money for the customer. How efficiently are funds being used? Is there anywhere that you can identify waste and leakage? What about staff productivity (yours and theirs)?

In fixed price contracts such as government-funded programs, there is a constant battle between how much money goes to service delivery and how much gets chewed up in administration. One of my clients delivers government-funded programs where most of the service users are located in regional areas. The contracts provide individual case management services, and as a result, the staff spend a lot of time on the road, travelling between service user locations, which costs not only time but money. One solution was to use Skype and GoToMeeting for most internal meetings and for some service user check-ins, cutting down on travel time without affecting a service user's experience. Options like this can never replace face-to-face contact entirely, but can be useful for some types of service delivery.

You can also examine the administrative workflow between your staff and the customer's staff. Are the reports you provide useful and timely? Do you get lots of one-off requests for information? If so, it might be good to look at how you can automate communication and reporting so that the customer knows when to expect information about the work you're delivering.

Improving service delivery

Once you've got the day-to-day friction out of the way, and you're managing the contract as effectively as possible, it's time to turn your attention to improving service delivery.

As the incumbent provider, you have a lot of knowledge about how the customer does business, and this can be extremely valuable in helping them do business better.

Many ideas can work here, and they will differ depending on your industry and the type of service you offer. Here are two examples.

In the printing industry, finding better ways to handle materials can be a productive way of improving service delivery. If you've ever been inside a high-speed printing factory, you know that high-speed printing presses are huge and chew up great quantities of raw material. Rolls of paper are taller than a person and as large as a redwood tree in circumference. There are enormous drums of printing ink and massive printing plates. Most of it is extremely heavy and none of it is easy to move around.

Procurement expert Craig Amos of PMP Limited, one of Australia's largest print manufacturing companies, explains that printing is a bit like food manufacturing. There's a recipe that needs to be followed in order to get a predictable result. Paper, ink and plates together equate to more than 70 per cent of PMP's expenditure and these categories get daily attention in an attempt to find new ways to do things better.

Interestingly, to Amos, good service from a supplier often looks like no service at all.

"We want to get as close to the manufacturing of that product as possible, wherever it is globally – whether that's in Finland, in Germany or in China – and we want to be responsible for most of the logistics and materials handling and processing ourselves," Amos says. PMP works to take costs out of its own business so it can be a low-cost customer for the supplier to serve, and also looks at ways to reduce costs in the supplier's business and supply chain.

As we saw, large customers can be demanding and they usually have high expectations. This is actually a good thing for suppliers, because it will often push you to do things that create new benchmarks in your business – things you can introduce to other customers.

Bega Cheese, for example, worked with a large provider of engineering services and engineering equipment, which held different contracts with two of Bega's bulk cheese manufacturing sites. Both sites were managed separately, explains Adel Salman, and when it came time to re-compete, neither site was keen on the proposal first put forward by the supplier. As a result, the supplier risked losing at least one of the sites to another engineering firm.

Salman asked the supplier to come up with a more compelling whole of group proposition that would help Bega to run engineering at these sites more effectively.

"They are the experts," Salman explains, "and we wanted to leverage off their expertise. We weren't focusing on them reducing their rates, but [on] what additional value they could contribute."

As it turns out, there was quite a lot. The supplier came up with ways to help Bega save costs at both sites, suggested a new training program and new ways to improve reporting. They put forward a competitive proposal with a level of service they had never achieved before, and that became a benchmark for them with other clients. In the end, the supplier agreed that this was not only a valuable process for Bega, but also for its own business.

We are not always lucky enough to chance upon a customer willing to give us an opportunity to revise our offer, and one that has the goodwill to work with us until we get across the line.

As the incumbent supplier, you have access to the customer in a way that no one else has. Use the contract delivery period to go to the customer with new ideas all the time, and you really will be primed to win again.

Aside from defending your position, there is another good reason to do this. Continual improvement with existing customers is actually a cost-effective way to innovate and to grow your business.

The last word here goes to Skybridge's Michael Abela, who says: "The easiest way to embed yourself with a client is to innovate around their needs, because you're creating a barrier to entry for any other contractor, who then has to replicate and invest up to your level of delivery. Once you've built a relationship with a customer, you're innovating in an organic environment so you don't have the cost of having to innovate and then win."

Chapter summary – Operational Excellence and Continual Improvement

☑ **Continual improvement is an expectation** now that every organisation that delivers large contracts is quality accredited, or has a quality program with built-in continual improvement.

☑ **Don't wait until the end of the contract** to go to the customer with ideas for better ways to do things. The next contract is won while delivering the first one.

☑ **If innovation is like building a new home, continual improvement is more of a renovation project.** Small improvements can make a big difference to contract or service delivery.

☑ **Review your KPIs regularly.** Often, performance can be measured more accurately as delivery progresses and there may be ways to adjust and enhance your KPIs so that they provide better information for you and for the customer.

☑ **Improve contract delivery** by removing friction in the administration and communication process, and by looking for ways to enhance productivity.

☑ **Improve service delivery** by working with the customer to create new benchmarks in your businesses that you can introduce to other customers.

☑ **Continual improvement equals continual innovation.** Use continual improvement initiatives with existing customers as an organic and cost-effective means of nurturing innovation.

CHAPTER 6

Customer Advocacy

BUYERS AND SUPPLIERS ARE more disconnected from each other than ever before. It's an unintended consequence of the way that competitive tenders have changed the sales environment, and a pity for both ourselves and for our customers. Being part of each other's journey towards growth and prosperity can help both of us to compete better and do business better.

As Dave Crenshaw writes in his book *Invaluable*, "Every day, the market you work in – regardless of the industry – asks 'Are you invaluable?' Did you answer the question satisfactorily today? Well done. Get ready to answer it again tomorrow."

As we saw in Chapter 2, the sales process with a customer is never truly over. Despite this, we often engage haphazardly with the customer over the life of a contract won through competitive tender. There's the initial nervous energy when submitting the tender response, a flurry of work when getting the contract set up and then a flat line of delivery over the course of the contract until the fever of the Request for Tender hits again.

Ideally, once we have built innovation, best practice and continual improvement projects, we want the customer to know about them.

This means a series of 'mini-pitches' throughout the term of the contract, led by the contract delivery team – the people who are closest to the customer and positioned best to put your ideas in front of them.

In engineering and project management – industries where you're only as good as your last job and every job must be won as a separate project – constant contact with customers is essential for long-term growth and success.

Nik Kilis, Business Development Manager for Arup in Australasia, brings in around $30 million worth of engineering business in Victoria alone each year. This often requires patient, long-term relationship building over many years before projects are put to market.

Nik is only one person in a business of 1200 people. As in most technical businesses, the challenge is to get senior technical experts – who love their projects – to give equal love to their customers and enjoy the thrill of winning the work. In a professional services market like engineering, the individual employee's brand is therefore as important as the corporate brand.

"Customers will 'buy' the corporate brand, but only because it is there to support the individuals who will be delivering the service," Nik explains. "When people personify the brand, this is what wins the work."

In the Introduction, I explained that when business-to-business markets became heavily procurement driven, something interesting started to happen.

Customers now only want to talk to the senior people who sign the contract (the 'revenue owners') or the operations people who deliver the contract. If you are a revenue owner, you are responsible for making sure money comes in, customers stay where you want them, and that your organisation fulfils its mission, whether that's for profit or not-for-profit. Your title is probably CEO, Country Manager, General Manager, or Head of (Everything/Something Very Important).

As the revenue owner, you will probably be the Bid Leader for major contracts and customers too.

I've worked with lots of revenue owners over the years and most are delightful, charismatic, driven and motivated people to whom selling comes naturally.

It doesn't matter whether you're selling community service programs or telecommunications services – revenue owners understand that sales are the fuel that drives the business.

As a revenue owner, talking to customers, getting their trust and earning the opportunity to work with them is probably one of the top three things that occupies your brain every day.

The same cannot necessarily be said of the people in your delivery team, who would probably rather do the job than sell the job.

During the contract, the delivery team is your primary selling team

Your contract delivery team (as I'll call them for convenience) has a huge influence over how the customer perceives not only your performance, but also how you manage customer communication, best practices, continual improvement and innovation over the course of the contract. Because they work with the contract and the customer every day, they are also in the best position to identify how to bring in more revenue from the contract, or make more profit.

The foot in the door may have come from your bid, but your contract delivery team is responsible for keeping the door open. This means that, at the very minimum, your delivery team needs to be working hard every day to make sure you have a story to tell when you are preparing to win again.

If you're like many of the revenue owners I know, even after the contract is won you probably still feel like you're trying to carry the customer all by yourself. You'd love to put your contract delivery team in front of the customer more often, but you're scared of what they might say if you do. And never mind what might happen in person: the team's reports, emails and other written communications can also leave a bit to be desired. You might find that you have to step in and write (or rewrite) them yourself.

This isn't sustainable. These days, your contract delivery team is your primary selling team, and that means they need to step up into their selling role.

Too many incumbent suppliers leave customer value on the table, simply because they are not systematically investing in their contract delivery teams and helping them to lead, and not just manage, their relationship with the customer.

To put this in context, let's say you have a contract worth $5 million over three years and a team of ten responsible for managing and delivering key elements of that contract. Each team member therefore carries the risk for $500,000 of that revenue.

But it goes further than that.

- Let's say the contract profit margin is 25 per cent, but has the potential to grow to 30 per cent if continual improvement opportunities can be identified. This would deliver an extra $250,000 in retained profit over the course of the contract.

- By identifying and successfully pitching new projects and add-on work to the customer throughout the course of the contract, you could also add 20 per cent in revenue, or $1 million.

- By improving contract communication and your reputation for innovation, best practice and continual improvement, you increase your chances of retaining the contract at the next tender, now worth up to $6 million with a profit margin of 30 per cent.

From a contract worth $5 million generating $1.25 million in profit, you now have a contract worth $6 million that generates $1.8 million in profit, a difference of $1 million extra revenue and $550,000 extra profit. You also have a better chance of retaining it.

This is an investment well worth making, and it starts with developing your contract delivery team's confidence, clarity and communication skills

The people who work in contract delivery teams often come from technical or operational backgrounds and are usually good at what they do, and proud of it. But often, they're neither trained nor experienced in sales and customer communication.

Therefore, they get scared when they have to talk to the customer or put something in writing, because they are afraid that what they do or produce might reflect poorly on them.

As a subject matter expert, they realise that they are the authority in what they do, but often resist sharing what they know because they don't know how to articulate it.

Whether you're aware of it or not, the customer is mentally marking your team on every interaction

Each interaction is an opportunity either to impress, or to confuse and alienate. It's like each team member is sitting an exam every time they come into contact with the customer – and they don't even know it.

Nowadays, with so much customer communication done in writing in the form of reports, emails and proposals, the risk of damaging a relationship through poor communication is greater than ever before.

Many technical and operational people in contract delivery teams either don't consider themselves 'communicators' or they've been taught to communicate in a way that's very factual.

There are seven primary communication strategies that individuals in contract delivery teams tend to demonstrate, from the least resourceful to the most resourceful:

- obfuscation

- repetition

- reporting

- analysis

- insight

- influence

- authority.

The least resourceful is **obfuscation.**

Obfuscation is the act of intentionally masking what we say and making it confusing, ambiguous and difficult to interpret.

Over the years I have seen a few senior, experienced technical people do this, both in person and in writing. In the people you manage, you might recognise this as an attitude of: "I don't want you to know what happened", or "I don't want you to know what I know".

Obfuscation generally comes from a place of fear – the fear that our knowledge is the only value we have in the organisation and that sharing it will reduce our power in some way.

Back to the customer, who is mentally marking your team on every interaction. Let's say they give marks out of 10.

Obfuscation gets a score of minus 10. Fortunately, only a very small number of people in contract delivery teams actually communicate in this way.

Slightly better than this, but still not very helpful for a customer, is **repetition**.

This is where someone in the team has identified a way of doing or saying something that has worked for them in the past, and then trots this out every time.

Look for the prevailing attitude of: "This is what probably happened, based on something similar that happened before."

In the eyes of the customer this scores a zero. Customers are paying for a service and effectively paying that person's wages, and this response isn't targeted to the customer's needs or wants. Although it doesn't come from a place of fear the way obfuscation does, repetition definitely comes from a place of disinterest and the customer feels the lack of energy and attention to the problem.

Generally, not too many people in contract delivery teams communicate through repetition, but combine them with the obfuscators and we've got a small but significant number potentially operating with a very unhelpful communication style that could damage your brand with the customer.

The most common communication strategy that contract delivery team members demonstrate is **reporting**. This is a very factual way of communicating, where the prevailing approach is: "This is what happened. That's all I need tell you and it's all you need to know."

Many people adopt this style because it's what they are taught in technical and on-the-job training. Unfortunately, this only rates five out of ten because it doesn't add any value to the customer's world. It probably doesn't tell you anything that you can't see yourself, and it certainly doesn't apply any kind of expertise to the problem.

Slightly better than this, but still not quite where you want to be, is **analysis**.

If analysis is your contract delivery team's primary communication style, then not only are they saying: "This is what happened," but also adding "and this is why it happened".

This is encouraging, because it means they are able to lend their expertise to the problem. If some members of your team have advanced their communication style from reporting to analysis, they're getting an extra point from the customer, which has them sitting at about six out of ten.

By this point, we've reached the level of skill at which most contract delivery teams and their members are currently communicating.

It is worth noting that if we were in a competitive bid right now, and the customer's evaluation team had scored even one element of our proposal at six out of ten, we would probably lose the contract.

We must do better than six out of ten, and not only in bids, but also in everyday communication throughout the contract term.

So there is a real opportunity gap here too.

Figure 3: Everyone in your contract delivery team has the knowledge to be an authority, but some may need help to move beyond a factual style of communication.

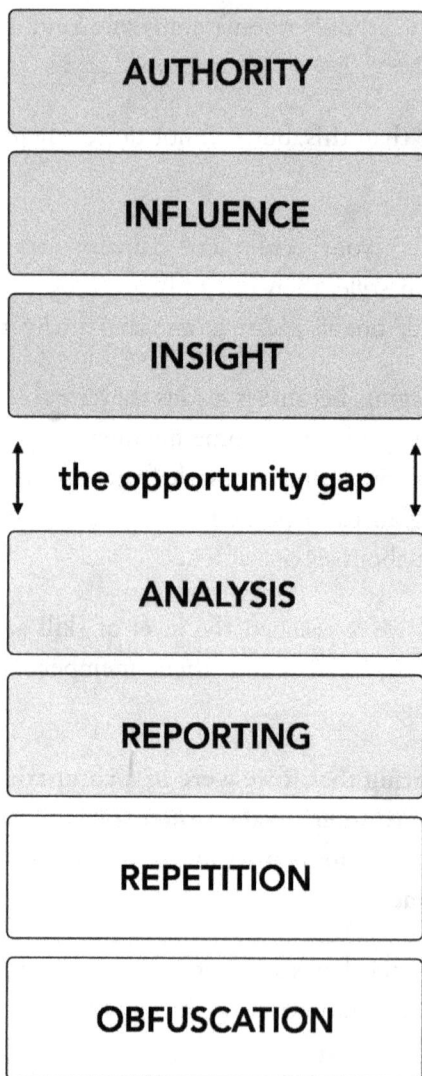

AUTHORITY

INFLUENCE

INSIGHT

↕ the opportunity gap ↕

ANALYSIS

REPORTING

REPETITION

OBFUSCATION

So let's look at the three levels above the opportunity gap, which represent the communication skills we want your people to aspire to and consistently demonstrate.

Much better than analysis are those who can provide **insight**. This means they are able to say: "This is what happened, and this is why it happened," and add, "and this is what it means for you."

Insight is extremely valuable for a customer, but not everybody who comes from an operational and technical background sees it as their role to provide insight. In fact, they may assume that the customer will read between the lines and come to this insight independently.

As a customer communication style, this wins you many more points – bumping you up to eight out of ten. But genuine insight is relatively rare.

Even rarer are those who have **influence**. Someone who operates at the influence level has already mastered the other communication styles. They are able to say: "This is what actually happened (reporting), this is why it happened (analysis), this is what it means for you (insight), and here is what I recommend you do about it and why (influence)."

When you achieve influence, you're probably going to be graded at nine out of ten by the customer. Very few contract delivery team members are capable of getting here and operating in influence as their default position without specific, targeted help.

If influencers have achieved a level of mastery in communication, then an **authority** is an absolute guru – someone who gets ten out of ten. When you're operating in authority, customers don't question you because they understand implicitly that you know what you are talking about.

Authority is a very powerful position, and this represents a huge opportunity for anyone in a contract delivery team who has ambitions to grow their status and their career. Every person in your team has the potential to be an authority and a decision leader, provided they are motivated and supported in a way that gives them the confidence, clarity and communication skills.

Recently, I was called in at short notice to work on a bid project for a large engineering company. They were hoping to retain their largest customer, whose business was due to go to tender in just a couple of weeks.

As part of developing our story for the tender, I worked with the contract delivery team to come up with 30 ideas for innovation, best practice and continual improvement projects that could be showcased in the proposal or rolled out during the course of the new contract.

Skills development wasn't part of the scope of my work with this team, and time was short, so as soon as the ideas were sketched out the team was given a template and a few instructions and went away to write their project briefs. When I got the project briefs back, six of them were brilliant, but the other 24 were not so good. The six brilliant briefs were written by the CEO, business development manager and marketing manager, all of whom understood the concept of how to sell an idea.

The rest were written by people in the contract delivery team, who had fantastic technical knowledge but who without exception struggled to make the connection between their ideas and the benefit to the customer. That's 80 per cent of projects where – without extra help – that great thinking could remain trapped inside the head of the contract delivery team, where it can't create any value for the customer.

When I do have the opportunity to do longer term work with an organisation, I love seeing the lights go on when those in the contract delivery team – who often don't think they can sell, and don't see it as their job to sell – realise what an enormous contribution they can make to a winning bid.

I'm really passionate about seeing that effect last when they get back to their day job, and giving them the tools, the techniques and the confidence they need to not only deliver the contract with excellence, but to generate continual improvement ideas and projects that help to grow and retain that client's business.

In my Client and Contract Leadership Program, I help contract delivery teams to find clarity around what they know, confidence in what they do, and the skills to communicate their value. One of the modules in this program is called Rev Up Your Reporting.

While it might be tough to get customers to read our blogs, newsletters and white papers, they will always read our monthly performance reports.

These need to reflect our sales and marketing communication agenda and also meet the customer's reporting expectations.

In the Rev Up Your Reporting module, teams are presented with nine topics that they could talk to the customer about, asked to think about what topics are most important to their own agenda this month, and to the customer's agenda, and then to plan their monthly reports around them.

Here is a snapshot of the topics we cover and that you and your team might want to consider to help you talk to the customer about the value you are delivering, now and in the future.

Nine Ways to Rev Up Your Reporting

New Initiative

Celebrate something you are working on that will create a new opportunity or solve one of your industry or client's deep problems. The primary purpose here is to demonstrate innovation, thought leadership and/or and market leadership.

In Our World

Showcase what you are doing for another client, perhaps in another industry, or another division of the customer's business that they may not be aware of. The primary purpose here is to demonstrate the breadth of your expertise and to position your team for future, similar work.

Warm Fuzzy

Describe a key staff member's job role, mark a long-standing team member's milestone, or share a staff success story. The primary purpose here is to connect the client emotionally with your team members. In complex services contracts, people are your primary saleable asset.

Opportunity Pitch

Put forward a case to be paid for something – either new or incremental work. The primary purpose here is to get some kind of 'advance' in your sales process: request a meeting with key stakeholders, book a presentation or demonstration, or get approval to proceed.

High Five

Acknowledge a great effort by the customer or their team. The primary purpose here is to 'catch the customer doing something right'. This helps to balance out the inevitable day-to-day friction between our team and the customer's team, and rewards behaviour on the customer side that helps us to achieve our goals.

Good News

Present a case study, good news story or share an example where you have gone above and beyond expectations when working with the customer or their clients. The primary purpose here is to show insight into the day-to-day workings of the contract, and highlight your service commitment.

Best Practice

Showcase a new initiative in the broader industry or profession and explain how you will adopt it. The primary purpose here is to show that you keep up with best practice in your profession and industry, and that through working with you, the customer gets access to the best and newest thinking on the market.

Problem Solved

Reveal a completed continual improvement initiative and show the difference it has made to the contract or service delivery. The primary purpose here is to show that your team is focused on improving day-to-day and not just delivering the baseline expectations of the contract.

Outstanding Result

Present a quantitative analysis of how you have exceeded your key performance indicators or other baseline expectations while delivering the contract. The primary purpose here is to make sure that this achievement doesn't get lost in the general reporting, and that it is elevated and applauded (as it should be).

Chapter summary – Customer Advocacy

☑ **Customers need and want to be engaged in our growth journey,** and to see how we are developing new ideas that can help them compete better and to do business better.

☑ **During the contract, your delivery team is your primary selling team.** However, most would rather do the job than sell the job, and need training and experience in customer communication.

☑ **The customer is mentally marking your team on every interaction.** It's like your team is sitting an exam every time, and don't know it.

☑ **Many technical and operational people have a factual, reporting style of communication,** because it's what they are taught to do in technical and on-the-job training.

☑ **The ideal is to be positioned as an authority,** and every person in your team has this potential.

☑ **While clients don't always respond to sales and marketing communications, they will always read our performance reports.** There are nine ways to Rev Up Your Reporting and get your agenda in front of the customer more consistently.

PART 3

Method and Mojo

Leading a successful bid when you already have the business means being responsible not only for the bid project, but also for the livelihoods of your staff and suppliers. In this section, learn how a successful Bid Leaders manage themselves, their teams and their organisations to make sure they win again.

CHAPTER 7

Beyond Ticking Boxes

BUYERS DON'T TURN SUPPLIERS into commodities. We do that to ourselves.

Price is just what buyers default to when suppliers haven't given them the information to make a better choice. We make it all about price when we don't have the courage to do something different and better than what others in our market are doing.

By now you have a series of projects to develop for your most important contract or customer. These focus on innovation, best practice, continual improvement and customer advocacy.

You're doing everything you can to reach 100 per cent effort on the factors that are within your control. You're building a better future for your customer and advocating to emerge as the clear winner when you need to bid for the business again.

Eventually that time will come, and your role will change from revenue owner to Bid Leader.

In these final chapters, we examine how to successfully fulfil your role as a Bid Leader when there is a tender document on the table, and how to bring your Ready to Re- compete Program to a successful conclusion.

Strategy, energy and delivery: what we need to bid for business successfully

Bid strategy represents what the customer most wants, what you can best deliver and what positions your organisation most favourably against competitors.

Energy and enthusiasm and are the fuel that powers a bid effort.

Delivery is the work you do to bring the bid strategy to life.

Each of these needs to be managed at three levels:

- Our own level as Bid Leader

- The team level, the people putting the proposal together, and

- The organisational level.

Only when all these levels are working together will the bid effort really feel like it is working.

Figure 4: Bid Leaders need to manage strategy, energy and delivery at three levels – organisational, team, and your own level as the primary power source

	STRATEGY	**ENERGY**	**DELIVERY**
BID LEADER	**Facilitate** Develop a competitive offer	**Role Model** Actively lead the project	**Drive** Implement the strategy
TEAM	**Articulate** Explore factors relating to customer, business & competitors	**Contribute** Even when working "five to nine"	**Collaborate** Success requires a team effort
ORGANISATION	**Commit** Agree to the strategy	**Reward** Provide recognition – win or lose	**Sponsor** Support the team and the strategy

Let's take a look at bid strategy first

Creating a bid strategy is like measuring up a custom-fitted suit. The finished product needs to perfectly fit the customer and take into account all of their preferences – both large and small – about how they want to do business with you.

To reiterate, bid strategy is about what the **customer** most wants, what **you** can best deliver, and what positions your organisation most favourably against **competitors**.

Getting this right is absolutely critical when you are the incumbent supplier, because the customer expects you to know them better than anyone else does.

Bid strategy is articulated through 'win themes', which I deliberately refer to as 'purchaser value topics'.

It's a subtle difference, but an important one. When we put time into thinking about what the purchaser will value, our ideas tend to be creative and generous, and more likely to help us win. The opposite of winning is, of course, losing, and when we use the language of 'win themes' we actually encourage thinking based on loss and scarcity.

As a Bid Leader, when it comes to strategy your primary job is to facilitate. You must hear all the ideas coming from the team and from the customer, and also have a point of view that balances competing opinions in order to develop the most competitive offer.

To facilitate bid strategy effectively, use a structured brainstorming process that will help you consider all the relevant factors. These include:

- what the customer wants

- what your organisation wants

- what the customer sees as value

- what you see as value

- influencers

- competitors

- what to promote

- what to combat.

The process I developed, use and teach is the Winning Words Bid Strategy and Purchaser Value Topics methodology.

Successful bid strategy facilitation requires the ability to hold the room in tension, allowing all views to be heard, without feeling the need for a quick resolution when there is dissent.

Bid strategy facilitation is not a pure facilitation role, as Bid Leaders are commercially responsible for the outcome. In a pure facilitation, the facilitator acts as a 'lubricant' to help a team resolve an issue or define a project, but typically does not contribute to the content or manage the project. In bid strategy facilitation, it can be tricky for a Bid Leader to manage their own vested interests and hold the room in tension in a way that achieves a balanced outcome.

It's important to avoid jumping too quickly to an obvious solution without going through the structured brainstorming first. Following this process means you are less likely to reach a self-serving conclusion that does not resonate with the customer's wants and needs.

If you find that this can be a problem for you, an experienced external bid strategy facilitator is a good investment. This makes it possible for you to contribute and act as part of the team during critical discussions about bid strategy, rather than having to run the process yourself.

At a team level, team members need to be able to articulate the strategy by sharing what they know is relevant about the customer, their own area of expertise and also competitors.

In creating the strategy for winning again, you need everyone who comes into contact with the customer to deliver their best thinking.

This means anyone who works at the coalface with the customer, including those who provide customer service and administrative functions, as well people in technical and operational roles, and also more senior people who can make commercial decisions.

Not all these people will be involved in writing the bid but all are important to creating the right strategy.

It's as though the most successful bid teams share a particular type of DNA. In very simple terms, DNA is a blueprint for how to build a living organism: it gives instructions to our cells about how they should grow and function.

A bid team is also a living organism – a group of smart people who come together to apply their skills and knowledge to developing a functional solution that will win or retain an important contract.

Bid teams need the right mix of customer and technical experts, balanced by a Bid Leader with the authority to make commercial decisions, and the skills to draw out the best ideas and drive the organisational change necessary to win.

What often happens, though, is that it's left up to the customer experts – the sales team – to run bids on their own. Customers have expectations and the sales team knows all about them: they will happily tell you what they are. Without the leadership and authority to implement these expectations, or the technical know-how to configure the systems and processes of the organisation to suit the customer, this knowledge remains under-used.

Figure 5: the DNA of a successful bid team contains the right mix of specialists with commercial, technical and customer expertise

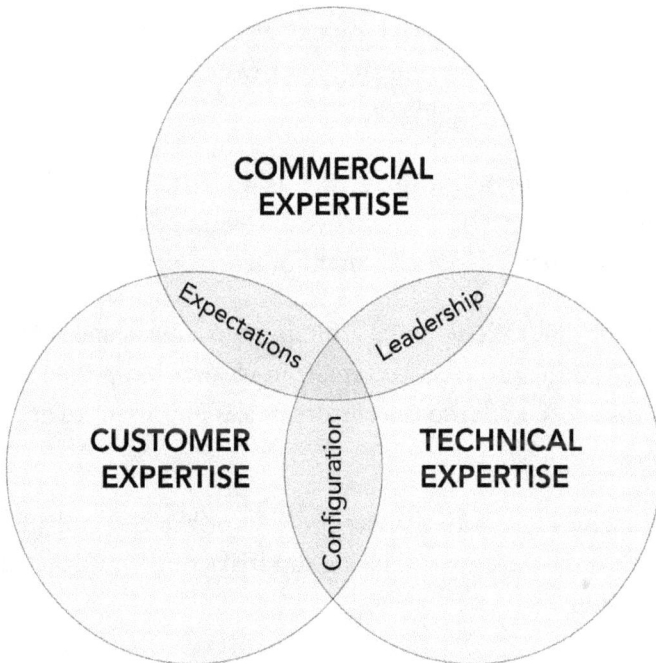

Building your team with the right mix of people creates a meeting of minds that will help you anticipate what the customer most wants, what you can best deliver and what best positions you against competitors at the time you make your bid.

As you can start to see from this diagram, it's at the intersection of these specialities that the magic truly happens. Customer experts provide information about customer expectations, which the commercial experts use to provide leadership to the technical people, who can configure a solution for the customer.

Avoid letting senior leaders outside your team hijack the bid strategy, particularly if they don't know the customer well or haven't worked at the coalface for a long time. Often these people dominate the discussion with commercial concerns and big-picture competitive strategy, at the expense of valuable customer and technical insights, and can make disastrous decisions that undermine the good work of the people who really know what is going on.

Finally, the organisation's role is to commit to the bid strategy, whether it is to deliver something different, build something new, or commit staff or other resources in a new way.

A bid or tender response is a binding document and you will be held to the promises you make in it. Your bid proposal sets out your entire offer to the customer. It is important to get this right.

Too many organisations over-promise in the bid and under-deliver on the contract, causing dissatisfaction and damage to reputation.

Buyers are tired of suppliers making promises that they don't follow through with. So always cost your bid promises and ensure that your organisation can keep them. Get commitment and sign-off internally before submitting your bid. Avoid making extravagant promises that you don't really intend to keep. Assume these promises will become part of your contractual responsibility to deliver.

Recently, I've been working on a large government services bid. Normally these things are very prescriptive, but this one is different. This time, the Request for Tender just says that any claims that tenderers make against the selection criteria will be included in contracts, and will form the basis for how their performance is judged. This is a neat and simple way of making suppliers responsible for what they promise, so expect to see more of this type of language coming through in tender documents.

For suppliers, even remembering what we have promised can be very challenging, particularly when the bid cycle takes so long to complete. When we spoke, Skybridge's Michael Abela was inking a deal that had taken two years from Request for Tender to resolution. This was a cycle of "sprints, then waiting" he says. For Abela, the biggest challenge was maintaining his knowledge of what happened during the last sprint and its associated meetings.

"When a procurement manager is sitting in front of you saying, 'Six months ago that widget cost $47,' you've got no idea what you said six months ago because you've lived a different life and sold other deals [since then]," says Abela.

To help him with this issue, Abela keeps detailed notes and meeting minutes, including minutes of internal meetings in which key decisions are made. This captures the reasoning behind each point of negotiation, making it easier to recall, for example, whether the costing relies on a discount offered by another supplier, or whether system development is needed.

"The linkages between the meetings are really important. When you've got that, it quickly re-engages you and brings you [into the present moment for] the current meeting. Otherwise, bid promises can become very expensive to deliver," Abela explains.

Energy: an essential, but often underestimated ingredient of a winning bid

Enthusiasm and energy are the fuel that powers a bid effort.

Because we are selling services, the amount of energy and enthusiasm we display for doing the job is directly correlated to the likelihood that the customer will give it to us.

This applies to winning again even more than it did in the initial bid, because the customer already knows us well and expects to see our personalities reflected in what we present.

As the Bid Leader, your role in generating energy and enthusiasm is to be a role model.

The amount of enthusiasm your team and organisation will display for a project, customer or contract directly correlates to how you feel about them yourself. Is this something you really want to win? What will it mean for your role, your team or your business if you win? What about if you don't? What are the great things that will happen if you win? What are the consequences of a loss?

Customers want to engage with real people who love what they do, not bland, faceless, corporate drones, so bid leadership is an active project leadership role where it is important to lead by example.

As a Bid Leader, you are neither a figurehead nor a taskmaster. You need to be right in there, actively working with your team and supporting them when they need it most.

When you do, you will find that your energy and enthusiasm are contagious. Make sure that you share your views widely among the informal power networks inside your organisation so there is a groundswell of support for what you are doing. Enlist the help of other line managers, if you need to, to get help with your projects and extra resources to cover for you and your team while you are deep in delivery of the bid. It's fine to ask your team to work longer hours on project delivery or bid delivery, as long as you are doing this yourself. Use the opportunity to give your people extra responsibility and make sure they are rewarded for it.

The team's role in generating energy is to ensure each member makes an individual contribution.

Successful bids depend on the delivery of a compelling offer, a sharp price and a great-looking proposal that is well written and interesting to read.

But each of these things is highly dependent on the energy, enthusiasm and creativity your team brings to the project. Without these, your proposal efforts can really struggle.

Delivering job satisfaction to the bid team – as well as a winning bid – can be a challenging task for a Bid Leader.

Bid teams often operate outside traditional reporting lines and boundaries, and team members are usually stretched, hassled and working on the bid as well as their day job.

When your people bring the best of themselves to working on a bid, they are more likely to do their best, most inspired and most creative work. Without their energy, there is a real risk that the proposal will lack personality and be flavourless and dry.

In a *Harvard Business Review* piece about job sculpting, Timothy Butler and James Waldroop explain that job satisfaction depends on how well the job reflects the individual's "deeply embedded life interests". These are long-held, emotionally driven passions, intricately entwined with our personalities. While life interests may not determine what we are good at, they do guide us toward the kind of activities that make us happy.

"At work, that happiness often translates into commitment. It keeps people engaged, and it keeps them from quitting," say Butler and Waldroop.

The principles of job sculpting can help bid teams too. If you have a person on your team with a passion for something specific, like designing a technical solution, let them get on with it. Another person, who loves seeing things done correctly, might get satisfaction from form filling, project management and production tasks.

Knowing what people's preferences are and the jobs they would enjoy doing – as opposed to the jobs that just need to be done – is an important role for a Bid Leader. When everybody is working on what they are great at, and what they love to do, the energy and enthusiasm that the team contributes will elevate the quality of the proposal.

Also, unless they're a Grand Prix pit crew, most teams and people don't do their best work under extreme deadline pressure. It's important to have empathy for the fact that for many people in the team, proposals are extra work on top of an already heavy load.

The other day, I talked with a program manager, Cameron, who works for one of my most successful clients. He hit the nail on the head when he said: "Bids are not a nine-to-five job for me. They're a 'five-to-nine' job."

Cameron isn't complaining. In fact, he is proud that his contribution helps his company to win work. But like many people who have an operational role and valuable knowledge, bids aren't part of his job description. They are something that gets done on top of everything else he needs to achieve in a day.

Spare a thought for the Camerons in your world. These are good people with a great work ethic, but their reserves of goodwill eventually run dry. When the next big thing comes up (after the last big thing) many are inwardly groaning. "Geez, another bid? I'd really like some time with my kids. I'd love to get to the gym. It's been ages since my wife and I went out to dinner."

Deadlines create pressure to get the work done, but not to do the best work. The best work comes from active thinking, planning and execution – well before the deadline. That's why it's so important to get your Ready to Re-compete Program sorted out well before the Request for Tender hits.

Energy generates more energy, and when each individual contributes their best efforts, the energy in the room will really power the team along.

On the other hand, even one team member being negative or withholding their best effort or knowledge can drain energy very quickly.

The organisation's role in generating the energy to power the bid is to reward and celebrate the team's work and effort – win or lose.

Rewards and recognition set up the expectation of success.

Teams need to be inspired to do their best work on bids, but it's more than likely that everyone is working on the bid as well as their day job. Worse still, often there are no thanks or recognition for contributing to bids: all the team sees is a mountain of thankless work they don't get paid for, which eats into their personal time. Those precious resources, enthusiasm and energy, are rapidly depleted by the way we handle bids.

In his book *Game Changers* — which couples the science of motivation with the power of game design — Jason Fox talks about the importance of inherent motivation. When an activity is inherently motivating, he says, we do it for its own sake. For the enjoyment it provides, the learning, development and growth it permits, or the feeling of accomplishment it creates.

According to Fox, people who find a task inherently motivating are more likely to be immersed in the activity – meaning they're giving careful attention to what they are doing and maintain awareness of the complexities, inconsistencies and integrations that will affect their success.

When it comes to bids, rewards and recognition really should result from effort – independent of whether you win or lose. Nothing pops the motivation bubble faster than unfulfilled expectation.

Many years ago, I worked on an important bid for a services organisation. There were at least 20 of us on the team and for six weeks we were pretty much chained inside a room. It was a nice room and there were pastries, and someone came to bring us coffee every now and again, but still. The team included outsourced specialists like me, and junior people from the organisation. It was very difficult to get the senior associates or leaders' time and most of us didn't have a clue what we were writing about. I felt for the internal staff – it was high-pressure work, with long hours. But they took it on enthusiastically because they hoped to work on the account, with a high profile, multinational company.

I will never forget the celebration lunch that the organisation put on to reward us for our hard work. We were waiting for the senior leaders to return from lodging the bid, and expecting cheers and high fives all round. Eventually they did arrive, late, with faces like thunder. It turned out we had been asked to pull out of the bid due to a last-minute competitive conflict. It was over before it had even begun.

The energy drained out of that room faster than a sinkhole can swallow a truck. Tim, the staff member sitting next to me who had been working overtime for weeks and missed his son's basketball final, was absolutely gutted. It was obvious that the lunch we were about to eat (mostly in silence) just wasn't enough to reward Tim for everything he had invested.

In *Game Changers*, Jason Fox explains that the keys to engagement and motivation are challenge, stimulation and reward. If there's no challenge, skills get blunt. If there's no stimulation, we get bored. And if there's no reward, we get burned (just like Tim).

So think about the rewards that your organisation can offer your people in return for all their work and effort.

While it's common to give time off after a bid to compensate for the extra workload, a much better way to generate energy and enthusiasm is to give your team at least part of this time off in advance. These few days could just mean the difference between a proposal that really hooks the customer, and one that lies there as lifeless and exhausted as the people who wrote it.

Technology employer Atlassian noticed that new staff members often came into their organisation tired and burned out from their previous job. To solve this problem, they now offer staff a 'pre-cation' (paid holiday) before they start with the company.

This is a great way to make sure that people arrive at work charged up and ready to go. According to *The Age* newspaper, Atlassian is now considered an employer of choice in an industry where competition for talent is high, and regularly rates a mention on lists of 'best places to work' in both the United States and Australia.

After the bid is completed and lodged, a celebration lunch or dinner for the team is a nice idea, but perhaps include an invitation – and gifts – for the life partners your staff have been neglecting all this time. Other options that are simple to organise include days off in lieu for the extra time they've worked, internal thanks and recognition, and a personal 'thank you' from the CEO.

Higher value options that may be more challenging to get across the line, but are still worth considering: promotions and new job titles; financial rewards, including pay rises, success bonuses and paid holidays; and public announcements or press releases thanking the individuals by name.

Finally, let's talk about delivery – the last piece in the puzzle

Delivery brings the bid strategy to life. However, delivering a convincing and competitive bid on time and on message isn't easy.

For starters, there's the Request for Tender to contend with, and the need to deliver a bid that complies with the instructions so that it doesn't fall at the first hurdle.

Building a bid is like building a house. I've been lucky enough to build my own home twice in my life. It's both one of the best and most challenging experiences I've ever had, in much the same way that bidding for business can be.

Everything that everybody says about building a house is true. It's time consuming, it's stressful, and things will go wrong. Things will be built the wrong way and you will have to make compromises.

A major reason why building both a home and a bid is so stressful is that people just don't follow the damn instructions.

I was walking past a building site recently and overheard a group of builders debating how to put something together on the home that they were constructing. An older man, who might have been their supervisor or foreman, stood back from the argument. Eventually he spoke up and said: "Guys, why don't we look at the plan?" All the builders laughed uproariously and one of them actually said: "The plan! That's for losers."

This is often the way incumbent suppliers feel when the Request for Tender comes out. It's your account – you live it and own it, but the Request for Tender is the customer's plan, not yours, and it's the customer's instructions that you have to work through, just like everyone else.

As I mentioned earlier, it's very important that incumbents do their best to subdue this discontent, respect the tender process and submit a bid that is compliant and respectful of the instructions. There is a time for negotiation, but this is the time for following the plan (the Request for Tender) and showing that we can do what the customer has asked us to do. On the other hand, though, focusing too much on the tender questions and schedules – particularly where this comes at the expense of the story and strategy – encourages conformity, and conformity is the enemy of any incumbent who wants to emerge as the clear winner.

Throughout this process, think of yourself as the master builder of a luxury, bespoke home. You're not a volume builder like everyone else. Your hard-earned expertise and your experience with the customer and the work you did in your Ready to Re-compete Program means you've already built the best possible offer, because you know the customer better than anyone else. Anyone can package up an assembly line quote or proposal and throw it out the door, but it's the love, care and craftsmanship that you put into delivering your offer that will make the difference.

The Bid Leader's role in delivery is to drive implementation of the strategy, and make sure the bid sells the story.

You have held the torch for this customer, from the beginning of your Ready to Re-compete Program to the development of your final bid strategy.

This is where it all comes together. Your role is to make sure that the bid says everything you need it to say, and reflects what you've worked hard to build in your Ready to Re-compete Program, while also being compliant with the instructions.

As you bring it all home, keep your optimism high and enthusiasm strong. Coach, encourage and support your team right to the end. Stand strong in your conviction that you have the winning offer and don't let the fear of being in a high stakes environment trip you at the final hurdle.

Remind yourself that you are doing this in service to the customer, to meet their needs and exceed their expectations. Believe in yourself and your team, and what you have to offer. Remember what the customer stands to gain from continuing to do business with you.

Two of my interviews with successful suppliers for this book were with the business development leaders of organisations in the not-for-profit sector. Both organisations, ACSO and Job Futures, are very successful in delivering complex government-funded services.

Not-for-profits have to fight hard for every last dollar they get. The sector is highly competitive and there is a growing trend towards rationalisation of smaller providers in favour of larger providers.

The dollars they fight for, however, aren't small at all. Some of the bigger not-for-profit organisations manage very large operating budgets, often aggregated from multiple funding streams across different government departments and programs. The lion's share of their operating budgets often come from state or federal governments through competitive bids, tenders or grant submissions. Each bid can result in the gain (or loss) of funding worth tens of millions, or hundreds of millions. As a result, there is a growing sophistication in this sector around resourcing and managing bids.

Kary Macliver is responsible for delivering 50 bids on behalf of Job Futures, which is looking to maintain and grow its business in the Employment Services 2015 funding round. Commonwealth Employment Services is an outcome-based program that has a 300-page Request for Tender and gives providers less than 20 pages per bid to respond. There is huge complexity in delivering 50 bids under these conditions, all tailored to their local region, and I worked with Kary and her team on their Ready to Re-compete Program for more than a year before the Request for Tender was released.

Kary recalls a time where she realised exactly how enormous the bid was. Multiplying the projected annual revenues in a contract that would hopefully run for five years with a possible five-year extension, the bid had a potential value of up to $1 billion.

Huge numbers like this can seem unreal at best, and terrifying at worst, and it's important not to let this get in the way of doing your best work.

Job Futures is founded on the principle that community organisations are best placed to deliver the services and solutions that work for their own communities. As a result of a change in government buying preferences, many small organisations are now leaving the employment sector. In a recent disability employment tender, Kary says, approximately 60 community contractors (which were not part of Job Futures) lost their contracts.

Job Futures sees its role as supporting community organisations – their members – to continue doing the great work they were built to do. This is a strong motivator for Kary and her team to deliver the best possible bids they can, using all the resources available to them.

"As an organisation whose goal is to put people in work and keep them in work, to keep our own members and their people in work is a real driver for everyone on the bid team," she says. Staying true to this conviction motivates Kary in what is a very challenging bid leadership role.

The team's role in bid delivery is to collaborate. Successful bids – and particularly bids to retain an existing piece of business – are truly a team effort.

In *Game Changers*, Jason Fox discusses the need to "make progress visible". I love his metaphor of a half-empty packet of Tim Tam biscuits as a progress bar (so that's why I always feel compelled to finish them!).

Inside your organisation, how can you raise the visibility of the work that you and your team are doing to retain your most important customer? What are the internal communication channels you can use to let people know what you're working on, the successes and challenges you're having, and encourage others to think about how they can help?

There is often a long stretch of time between the genesis of an idea and its conclusion. Helping people see the progress they've made on their Ready to Re-compete projects can generate a sense of accomplishment and pride in the work.

When the Request for Tender lands and you're in the middle of working on the bid itself, find a way to make everyone's best contribution visible. There's nothing like the walls of your bid control centre ('war room') for this purpose. Paper your walls with pictures of the decision makers, together with the outcomes they want to see and the language they want to hear. Put up all the flipchart notes from your strategy sessions so that everyone can see what they are supposed to be working on. Draft and circulate your executive summary early so everyone in the team can contribute their best examples, explanations and evidence.

It's a good idea to get your team working together in the same room, at least for part of the time, if at all possible. This forces people away from their business as usual to-do lists and helps them to prioritise their work on the bid. Try not to let people work from their desk during critical content creation periods, particularly straight after bid strategy and content planning sessions when the material is freshest in their mind and their motivation is at its highest. Otherwise the siren call of the day job will lure them away every time and you will have to chase them for late, rushed or unfinished material until the cows come home.

Last, but certainly not least, the organisation's role in bid delivery is a sponsorship role.

A sponsor assumes final responsibility for another person or thing. As the bid's sponsor, the organisation itself has an important role to play in helping steer the project to a successful conclusion.

Practical support for the Bid Leader and bid team from across the organisation include: freeing people from non-essential work so that they can fulfil their projects and other tasks in the bid strategy; encouraging other teams and individuals to generously contribute their expertise and knowledge when asked; and practical resources, from meeting rooms, lunch and coffee to additional funds for proposal support.

When bid teams are under-resourced and expected to operate without extra time or budget, quality and commitment suffers – and so does the outcome. So don't be stingy with your bid team. Take the lock off the war room fridge. Buy lunch, shout them coffee, bring in pastries. Show them the love and they will show you the money.

Chapter summary – Beyond Ticking Boxes

☑ **Delivering a successful bid means managing strategy, energy and delivery.** These need to be managed at three levels – our own level as Bid Leader, and at the team and organisational levels.

☑ **Creating a bid strategy is like measuring up a custom-fitted suit.** Bid strategy represents what the customer most wants, what we can best deliver and what positions us most favorably against competitors. The result is a perfect fit.

☑ **Successful bid teams share a particular DNA,** balancing customer, technical and commercial perspectives.

☑ **Energy and enthusiasm power a bid effort.** When selling services, the amount of energy and enthusiasm we display for the job is directly correlated to the likelihood that the customer will give it to us again.

☑ **For many people, proposals are not a nine-to-five job – they are a 'five-to-nine' job.** It is important to recognise and reward effort, as well as success.

☑ **When the stakes are high, keep your chin up.** Coach, encourage and support your team right to the end and stand strong in your conviction that you have the best offer to win again.

CHAPTER 8

Bid Leadership: Building Your Mojo

BID LEADERSHIP IS A high-stakes job. Do it well and you will catapult your career into the stratosphere.

During interviews for the book, I asked business development leaders to tell me, on a scale of one to ten, how intimidating they find it when they need to re-compete for an important piece of business.

Most rated it an eight or nine – no matter how confident they are in their ideas, growth plans, and track record – due to the keen sense of responsibility they feel for the people whose livelihoods are at stake.

In the last chapter we discussed why energy and enthusiasm are the fuel powering a winning bid.

As Bid Leader, you're a primary provider of energy to your team. Your power-up sources are the confidence you have in your skills, coupled with the offer that you've been building through your Ready to Re-compete Program.

According to the Oxford Dictionary, the word 'mojo' originally meant a charm or a spell, but now it's more commonly used to mean sex appeal or talent.

While it's pretty difficult to feel sexy when you're in an environment that can be this intimidating, your natural talent has led you this far. And there are some simple things you can do to boost your mojo.

In this chapter, we unpack some of the critical skills and techniques you can use to build your confidence and effectiveness as a Bid Leader.

When there's a tender document on the table, you need a simple and proven methodology to follow that focuses your time, your energy and your effort where they are most needed: on what will help you win.

As soon as the Request for Tender is released, you will only have a short period of time, most commonly four weeks, to put your entire submission together.

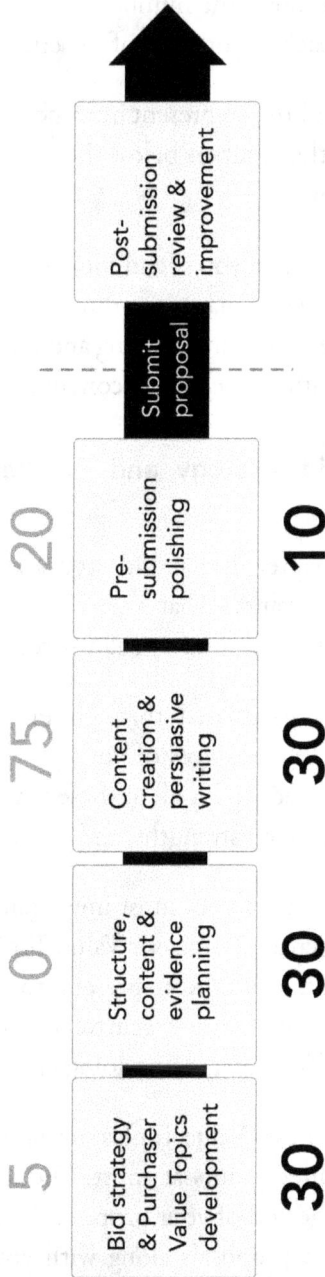

Figure 6: Clear winners spend their bid development time on strategy and planning work that will help them win (bottom line), where others spend too much time on lower-value tasks like writing and re-writing (top line).

In the diagram above, the numbers represent the percentage of time spent on each major stage of the critical bid period.

Those above the boxes represent how most people usually divide their time and the numbers below show where the clear winners spend their time.

As you will see, when you spend more of your time articulating your bid strategy and planning your content and evidence, you will need to spend less time writing and even less re-writing, and you'll end up with a much more convincing proposal.

Stage 1 – bid strategy and Purchaser Value Topics development

We saw in Chapter 7 that bid strategy represents what the customer most wants, what you can best deliver and what positions you most favourably against competitors.

Bid strategy is articulated through Purchaser Value Topics, which are the key messages of your proposal. To be effective, every message needs to hit all of these marks – it represents the customer, it sells your strengths, and it combats competitors.

As Bid Leader, one of your most important jobs is to help your team craft and create Purchaser Value Topics, as they will drive and underpin the offer you present to the customer. These also form the core of your executive summary, and later in the chapter we will look at a methodology for writing this.

Keep your Purchaser Value Topics simple and short — no more than two or three points at most. The idea is that when the buyer gets to the end of your proposal (remembering that they will assess many proposals along with yours) they can clearly articulate the two or three main reasons why they should choose you.

By the time the Request for Tender comes out, you'll have a good idea of what you're putting forward, thanks to your Ready to Re-compete Program and the projects you've been working on throughout the contract. While it can be difficult to negotiate many internal points of view, it is important to stay true to your vision if you want to be successful.

"You can't win with a muddied vision, watered down to keep everyone happy," says Kary Macliver from Job Futures. "Nowadays I say: 'this is what we have to offer and if they don't want that, then they don't want us'." This tactic has proven very successful for Kary and her team.

As we saw earlier, the DNA of a successful bid team incorporates a balance of commercial, customer and technical perspectives.

As Bid Leader, you represent all these elements, but in bid strategy will probably have the strongest voice on commercial considerations, including the discussion of competitors.

Mostly, we think of our competitors as the firms or organisations that are the closest match to ourselves – what I call 'peer competitors'. This is a dangerous assumption, particularly as an incumbent supplier, because we don't want to underestimate the field of competition and the other options open to the customer.

In my practice, and in delivering my Persuasive Tender and Proposal Writing Master Class, I've read and provided feedback to hundreds of people about their past proposals and tender responses. I look for evidence that the writer has thought about what competitors might be offering, and come up with ways to better promote their own strengths and combat the strengths of competitors as a result.

Unfortunately, very few proposals adequately address the issue of competition.

We are not selling in a vacuum, and in a competitive tender the buyer will consider many proposals along with yours – maybe a handful, or maybe hundreds.

Getting your head around what others might be offering is also a good way to test the validity of your own offer and ideas.

Aside from peer competitors, here are some ways to think about potential competitors that might pose a threat to your ability to win. Start by making a list of all the competitors you can think of, and consult your team to make sure you have covered them all.

Where is your competition going to come from?

- National organisations, if you are local.

- Local organisations, if you are national.

- Much larger or much smaller organisations.

- Organisations that already work with your customer in another capacity.

- Organisations with expertise in an area of current or future interest to the customer.

- Organisations with expansion plans that include your market space.

- Potential partnerships among competitors, including joint ventures and consortia.

- Offshore and multinational organisations.

- The customer – they might do nothing, spend their money on other priorities, or decide to do the work in-house.

When you have a good idea of the real competition you might be facing, start researching and examining each competitor in depth.

- Who are they and what do they do?

- What is their current relationship with the customer? What other business do they have with them?

- What is in favour of them winning the contract? How can you combat their strengths?

- What could count against them? How can you exploit their weaknesses?

- Do they hold any 'trump cards' that could change the playing field in this bid? How can you counter these?

- What is the level of threat to you – low, medium or high?

It's essential to analyse competitors regularly, and even more important when you have a contract you don't want to lose. This work will give you some good insights into where you are placed in the market, and where you may need to strengthen your offer to win again.

Stage 2 – structure, content and evidence planning

Tender responses are prescribed format proposals. The structure of the Request for Tender – what it's asking for, and the order it's asking for it in – dictates the structure of your response.

When the Request for Tender arrives, you will be primed and ready ... and you have been waiting for a while. It's very tempting to get stuck straight into writing. However, this is a mistake.

After holding your strategy session, where you decide on your final Purchaser Value Topics, there are two additional things you need to do before you start to write.

The first is to draft your Executive Summary, which encapsulates the value of your offer. This goes at the very front of your proposal, in front of any questions or schedules the buyer has asked you to complete.

The second is to plan your content, including the evidence to support your claims, so your team can write good material.

When it comes to delivering a winning bid, getting it on paper is the toughest part, according to Karenza Louis-Smith of ACSO. "You can have the vision and the ideas, but when the specifications come out, you have got to somehow take all of that out of your head, and match it to what at times seem like bizarre questions," she says.

Over time, Karenza has learned that the "bizarre questions" are there for a reason, and the content planning process helps her and her team understand not only what the questions mean but also to decide if there is a match between what the customer wants to buy, and ACSO's vision to deliver. As a visual thinker, something that helps Karenza is to whiteboard the solution and to talk it through.

"We might spend half a day just drawing, redrawing, rubbing things out and putting them up again," she says, pointing to a large map of Victoria sketched on her whiteboard and containing three days' worth of recent work she has been doing with her team.

Executive Summaries

The executive summary is your proxy for a face-to-face conversation with the customer. It sets out your case for the business in a short, confident piece of less than three pages – no matter how long and complex your actual proposal is.

As the Bid Leader of the incumbent's team, your job is to make sure that the executive summary really rocks. Write it yourself, in a clear, confident tone of voice that sounds exactly like it would if you spoke to the customer in person.

Writing your executive summary straight after your bid strategy session with your team is a great idea. Your Purchaser Value Topics are the scaffolding on which you will build your offer, and writing your executive summary lets you climb up on that scaffolding, test how strong it is, and see where there are gaps you need to fill.

Here is a simple method to follow when you're writing your executive summary.

1.   Thank the client and name the project, contract or opportunity you are responding to.

2.   Show that you understand what the client is looking for, presenting at least several insights that go over and above the requirements in the Request for Tender.

3.   Include an offer statement that summarises your offer in one paragraph. Usually all you will need to do here is present the headline sentence for each of your two to three Purchaser Value Topics.

4.   Confirm that your proposal conforms to the Request for Tender requirements. If necessary and relevant, explain briefly how they should read the proposal.

5.   Using your Purchaser Value Topics as headings, explain why the customer should choose you. Substantiate claims with your best examples and evidence, and include testimonials. This section represents the bulk of your executive summary.

6.   If you haven't already, briefly explain why your proposal offers value for money. If relevant, address any concerns the client may have about choosing you.

7.   Ask for the business and summarise why you deserve it.

8.   Sign off using your name, as the most senior person on your bid team.

Content and evidence planning

A good process for content and evidence planning means you and your team will spend less time writing and rewriting. That means conserving precious energy.

Remember, even if you are the incumbent supplier, it's important that you don't take the customer's knowledge of you for granted. Tehara Wickham explains that at NAB, an evaluation panel might contain anywhere from five to eight different stakeholders. They will come from the business area you are pitching to, and possibly also from its technology, legal and environmental sustainability teams. There's a very good chance that not everyone on the evaluation panel will be familiar with your work. Your proposal needs to explain this, and provide examples and evidence to support what you are saying.

Sit down with your team after the bid strategy session and really examine each of the questions in turn. What are these questions really asking? Is there a question behind the question? What does the buyer really want to know? Are there potentially explosive issues here that you need to be aware of?

When thinking about how to answer each question, consider the major claims you want to make. **Claims** are the main points in your argument to win the business. For each claim, you will need to provide evidence.

Evidence is exceptionally important in a bid or tender response. In a tender evaluation, the people sitting on the evaluation panel have to give each part of your proposal a score. What sets apart high scoring proposals is the believability of their claims, which is determined by the quality of the evidence that the supplier provides.

There are two main types of evidence to look for:

- **Quantitative evidence** is something that can be measured numerically.

- **Qualitative evidence** is something that can be observed, but not measured numerically.

Figure 7: Evidence matrix for proposals

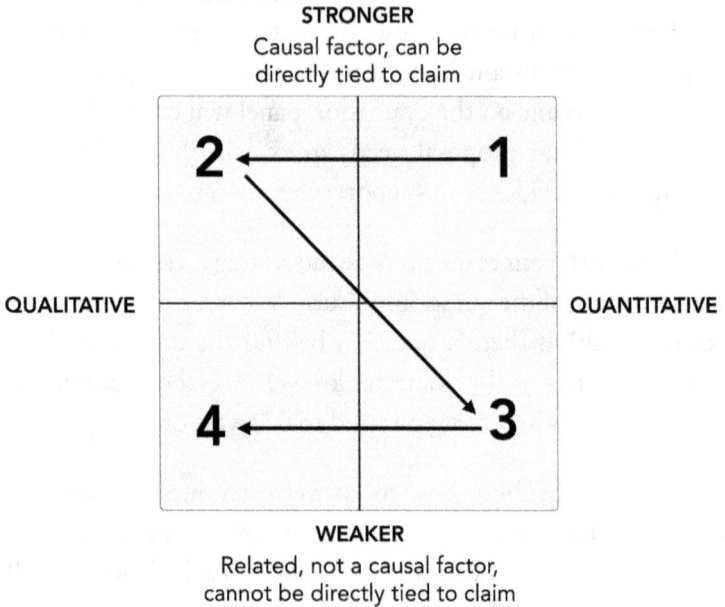

Not all evidence is created equal. The strongest evidence you have at your disposal is anything that demonstrates the direct results of what you did, and therefore can be directly tied to the claim. This evidence can be either qualitative or quantitative. Weaker evidence is something that might be related, but is not a direct result of what you did, and therefore cannot be directly tied to the claim.

For example, consider these two sentences, in which the supplier is attempting to substantiate a claim of **reliability**:

We supply more than a million widgets each year to 87 contract customers, including almost half of Australia's municipal authorities and eight of the country's top ten private cleaning contractors.

Our standard supply contract promises 98.5 per cent uptime for each individual widget, however, we have consistently exceeded this benchmark, achieving 99.3 per cent uptime over the past three years across all 87 contracts.

Both of these sentences provide quantitative evidence, but only the second provides strong quantitative evidence that can be directly tied to the claim of reliability. The fact that they do business with many customers is probably a good thing for overall customer satisfaction, but it may not be because of their reliability.

Both qualitative and quantitative evidence are important in a proposal, because humans make decisions based on gut feeling, but we justify them with logic.

In *Hooked – How Leaders Connect, Engage and Inspire with Storytelling*, Gabrielle Dolan and Yamini Naidu explain that facts are hard to remember because they lack emotion.

"It is very hard to get people on just the facts," Dolan and Naidu say. "As leaders, we need to create an emotional connection to ourselves and to our message by presenting the facts and also the feeling."

This is true in proposals as well. However, a tender is still a formal evaluation environment, in which the evaluation panel has to give you a score.

This means that it's good practice to present your strong quantitative evidence first, to tick the box, and make the human connection by immediately following it with your strongest qualitative evidence.

For example, in a tender response for facility maintenance services that asks for evidence of **experience** in similar contracts, the incumbent supplier might say:

> In addition to working with Sandy Beach Council, Neat as a Pin also has an excellent service record with neighbouring Seaforth Council, achieving 99 per cent compliance to KPIs against a benchmark of 97 per cent over six years. (Quantitative Evidence 1)

> "Neat as a Pin is my best and most reliable supplier. I highly recommend them to any council requiring a quality cleaning and facility maintenance service." Roger Smith, Seaforth Council Facilities Management Officer (Qualitative Evidence 2)

When it comes to collecting and documenting evidence, think about how you can do this over the course of the contract so it isn't a struggle when you come to the end, and so that good work isn't forgotten.

Scott Wright from NEC acknowledges that this is a particular challenge for him as a Bid Leader, particularly now that the contracts he manages are so sizeable and that bids also require input from NEC offices in other states. For Scott, part of maturing his process as a Bid Leader has been to collect quantitative and qualitative evidence over the life of the contract that will help him in his contract reporting and when he next needs to submit a bid.

Stage 3 – content creation and persuasive writing

As the Bid Leader, you probably won't do all the content creation and writing yourself (with the exception of the executive summary).

This task will mostly fall to your team and to any external suppliers working with you as part of subcontracting or partnership arrangements.

However, it's important to recognise good content and good writing when you see it, and to coach your team when their performance doesn't quite measure up to your high standards.

- To get good content for the proposal, first plan the content together, which you did at Stage 2. This sets a firm expectation about what you want the team to deliver.

- Tell the team that you expect original material, not something they've copied and pasted from the last proposal. When you're selling services, you're selling your expertise and knowledge. While it's ok to use existing source material for background, you want to see fresh thinking reflected on the page.

- Be clear in your own mind about the difference between descriptive and persuasive writing, and make sure the team is delivering the latter.

Descriptive writing just presents facts and information. Persuasive writing brings the reader around to your point of view. While descriptive writing is ok for some tasks, we're looking for persuasive writing in a proposal.

Proposal writing is not like essay writing, where you introduce your topic, explore it in the body of your essay and then deliver your conclusion. In proposal writing, your conclusion comes at the beginning of your writing. It's the conclusion you want the customer to reach, and the rest of the points underneath substantiate why they should reach that conclusion.

As we saw, for many technical and operational people in contract delivery teams, 'reporting' is their primary communication style. They will probably need some help to become persuasive writers. Encourage your team to take a point of view on what they're writing about and to start each piece with a sentence that summarises their main argument.

Content creation and persuasive writing are the part of the process that many people find the most challenging, and that's why it tends to chew up so much time and energy.

Here are some other things I've learned through working with successful bid teams that will help you with this part of the process.

Your best writers are always going to be your contract delivery team

In a proposal, what you say is more important than how you say it, and making sure the people in your team contribute their knowledge is very important. This means getting everyone involved in proposal writing, even if they don't see themselves as writers.

Some people will be more suited to writing proposals as a regular gig than others.

Responding to tenders can feel like you are sitting an exam every day of your life. People who were good at exams at school or university and who quite like the challenge of sitting exams (yes, it happens) are ideal for this type of work.

Bid writers need to quickly understand what's being asked for in a Request for Tender and know how to respond.

Likewise, getting good exam marks requires the confidence to understand and interpret unfamiliar questions very quickly and under time pressure. It means being able to plan a response that addresses that question, then identify relevant content and ignore stuff that isn't relevant, and weave an argument or point of view throughout.

A team member who has a good academic record with high exam scores in complex subjects is highly likely to be suited to the task of working on tenders. It doesn't really matter what kind of subjects they were good at, as long as the exams required a written answer.

Make sure your proposal personality matches your real personality

When we present in person, there are many cues that show our personality. In a written proposal, however, these cues are more limited. Personality mostly comes through in the way the proposal looks and feels, and of course in the way the proposal sounds when you read it.

There are two types of presentation to pay attention to in a proposal – visual and aural.

Visual presentation is about how the proposal looks and feels. Aural presentation is about how it sounds when the buyer reads it.

Let's think about aural presentation first. When you're the incumbent supplier and at least some members of the evaluation panel know your team, the more voices that come through in your proposal, the better. This demonstrates the size and scale of the team working on the bid, and that each one brings their unique perspective, personality and point of view.

Of course, this is an important bid. There is a lot riding on it. As a result, there are probably many people outside your team who want to be involved.

Don't let your marketing and communications department push you into letting their copywriters subsume your personality with glossy corporate speak to "make the proposal sound more professional/on-brand/speak with a single voice." Some smoothing and tidying up of the writing might be necessary (editing), but resist the lure of wholesale rewriting that only has the effect of flattening out the overall tone of your proposal.

Visual presentation is important, but not for the reason that your marketing people might think it is.

Competitive tenders are a crowded environment where a buyer assesses many competitive tenders at the same time – sometimes a handful and sometimes hundreds. If it's a public tender, it's a bit like 'cattle call' auditions in the entertainment business, and the same rules apply: show up on time, respect the judges, wear your biggest smile and most sparkly outfit. (Well, almost all the same rules.)

Quality presentation is a sign of respect for the process. This doesn't mean shiny stock pictures that show nothing of your personality. Use photos of your own staff. If an idea is still a work in progress, show it as sketch, rather than as a glossy diagram.

Sound approachable, but assertive

What do your proposals usually sound like to the customer? Matter of fact? Professional but detached? Approachable? Assertive?

Proposals are all about leading the customer's thinking to your point of view, and it's usually best to employ a combination of approachable and assertive tones when writing.

For example, in a tender for medical recruitment services, suppliers were asked to specify if they had any preferred supplier agreements with other customers. It's possible that the buyer did this because they were already thinking about the conflicts of interest these agreements might create, however they also might not have fully understood the implications.

My client, let's call them Medical Recruiters, took an assertive tone on the issue – it played to one of their key competitive advantages – and they needed to strongly influence the buyer's thinking. Their answer went something like this:

> Our market position, which is free of conflicts of interest, creates a compelling reason to consider Medical Recruit-ers as one of your preferred suppliers. Medical Recruiters does not have any preferred supplier agreements with direct

competitors of Pharma Co. Our only preferred supplier agreement is with ZedCorp, a large multinational medical device company.

There are real risks in appointing preferred suppliers of recruitment services that already hold such agreements with your direct competitors. For example, how does the recruiter decide where to send an excellent candidate, when they have two or three other clients looking for a similar person?

Where potential conflicts of interest do exist, it is important you are 100 per cent confident in the quality of the consultants who will be allocated to your account. The 'Best Practice in Human Resources Report' (date) surveyed 5000 professionals who changed jobs and found that the consultant was the main catalyst in building their enthusiasm for the role and gaining their commitment to the employer.

The argument convinced the buyer, and Medical Recruiters won a place on their preferred supplier panel.

Stage 4 – reviewing

As the Bid Leader, your job is to get maximum value at every point where the proposal is reviewed for feedback. Whatever you do, don't chew up your valuable time, or other people's time, acting as overqualified spellcheckers.

If you work in a large organisation with many layers of management – or if you are bidding in a consortium – get sign-off on your bid strategy early by circulating a draft version of your Executive Summary to your senior management and/or consortium partners. This will ensure you have approval of the strategy and key messages before writing starts.

The good news about reviews is that you shouldn't need to do too many. Once you've captured your offer through Purchaser Value Topics, and put the best possible material up-front through content and evidence planning, only two detailed reviews of the proposal should be necessary – first, and final.

At the Draft 1 review, you'll want to lead the bid team in a 'page turn' meeting to make sure the content reflects what was promised in the content plan.

In the final review, your role is to make sure that the final bid is compliant (follows all the buyer's instructions) and fully articulates your bid strategy. At this point, you might want to enlist the help of a peer reviewer – someone who hasn't been involved in the bid and can therefore act as a fresh set of eyes on the document. Ask them to ignore minor issues like spelling and formatting, as the document will be proof-read afterwards, and instead concentrate on message.

Once they've finished reading the proposal, ask them to explain in their own words, the two or three key reasons why the buyer should choose you. If what they say reflects what you want the buyer to hear, your work here is done.

Submission and presentation

Finally, you're ready to submit....with a smile on your face and a song in your heart.

You and your team have worked hard on this, not only for weeks, but hopefully also for months or maybe even years. First you prepared your Ready to Re-compete Program so you had something to sell, over and above your already awesome performance as the incumbent, and then you wrote the best darn proposal the customer has ever seen in their lives.

Once they've read it, of course, they will want to see you.

Here are some words of encouragement about the shortlisting interview.

A bid interview is neither a presentation nor a performance. It is a test of how prepared you are to deliver on your promises, and how well you know your stuff.

The real work of winning the bid was done when you put your offer together.

If you sold them on paper and they want talk to you, the interview isn't a pitch. It's a conversation about how you're going to do business together and maybe also to tie up one or two loose ends and clarify things that they didn't understand on the first pass.

As the incumbent supplier, this should feel natural and comfortable.

Because the stakes are high, and especially if it has been more than a couple of months since you submitted your bid, make sure you re-read it and are as familiar with it as the day you first wrote it. Assemble your A-team and practice before you go in.

If you feel you need extra confidence to make your interview more authentic, it's a good idea to set aside some time to practice with a colleague or a presentation coach. If you decide to take this path, understand that coaching on the mechanics of the presentation – making you a better presenter – is not going to push you over the line.

It's your offer that has sold them. And if you're sold on the idea yourself, you've got this. Go in and speak from the heart about what you know. Be authentic and don't try to be too clever.

Show up like a human being who wants to help another human being and the customer will love you for it. That's all they ever wanted, right from the beginning.

And last but not least – congratulations. It won't be long before you find out that you're winning again.

Time to celebrate, take a deep breath, and start all over again.

Chapter summary – Bid Leadership: Building Your Mojo

☑ **Bid Leadership is a 60/40 game:** spend 60 per cent of your time on bid strategy, content and evidence planning, and only 40 per cent on writing and reviewing. This reduces wastage and re-work.

☑ **Purchaser Value Topics, which are the key messages of your proposal, should be few in number – only two to three at most.** Their purpose is to help the buyer to remember and articulate the main reasons why they should choose you.

☑ **The Executive Summary is your proxy for a face-to-face conversation with the customer.** Draft it yourself, before the bid is written.

☑ **Substantiate all claims with evidence.** Quantitative evidence helps 'tick the boxes' in the bid scoring process, but qualitative evidence supports the 'gut feeling' that is also important to making a decision.

☑ **Your best writers are always going to be your contract delivery team.** Encourage them to take a point of view, and to write in a way that is both approachable and assertive.

☑ **Review, submit and present in full confidence that you've done everything it takes to win again.** By this time, you surely have.

Final Words and Next Steps

ROBYN HAYDON IS ONE of Australia's leading experts on business development, specialising in helping organisations win business through formal bids, tenders and proposals. Robyn is on a mission to bring creativity, energy and enthusiasm back to the process of winning and serving customers. Through her work, Robyn hopes to build a legacy of strong, capable businesses and individuals who see it as a privilege to work on bids and proposals, and who are empowered to bring the best of themselves to their business development role – no matter what their "other" roles may be.

- Book Robyn to speak at your next sales meeting, strategy retreat or conference

- Engage Robyn to help you build a Ready to Re-compete Program for your most important contract or customer

- Talk to Robyn about organisational bid capability building programs, including one-on-one mentoring for current and potential Bid Leaders

- Check out Robyn's public training programs, including the Persuasive Tender and Proposal Writing Master Class and the Persuasive Speed Writing Program

- Purchase Robyn's first book *The Shredder Test – a step-by-step guide to writing winning proposals*

- Subscribe to Robyn's weekly newsletter, The Winning Pitch

- Connect on LinkedIn or get in touch directly

www.robynhaydon.com

www.winningwords.com.au